GOT ANY GUM CHUM?

GIs in Wartime Britain 1942–1945

Helen D. Millgate

**Essex County
Council Libraries**

First published 2001
This edition first published 2009

The History Press
The Mill, Brimscombe Port
Stroud, Gloucestershire, GL5 2QG
www.thehistorypress.co.uk

British Library Cataloguing in Publication Data.
A catalogue record for this book is available from the British Library.

ISBN 978 0 7524 5023 0

Typesetting and origination by The History Press
Printed in Great Britain

Contents

The 373rd FG at Woodchurch, Kent, being briefed before a raid on northern France. (Kent Messenger)

Bombing up Little Chris, somewhere in Kent. (Kent Messenger)

Acknowledgements

My particular thanks go to Ken Wells and Vince Hemmings, who have been so extraordinarily generous in providing me with photographs and information. Also to John Costello, Jules Honig, Eddie and Hilda Graham and Stan and Betty Kieffer in the USA who have corresponded with me at length, as has Stanley Freestone from Sussex. Mrs Vincent of the Royston Museum has been very helpful. I am extremely grateful to all those people who replied to my request for information, in Britain, the USA, Australia and New Zealand:

Sheila Anderson, Joan Andrews, Mrs B. Blachford, Mr and Mrs Dennis Bolam, Reg Bossom, David Brinsden, Margaret Brown, A.T. Bulgen, Howard W. Campbell, Peter Canovan, Mrs B. Carter, J. Chainey, Betty Channing, John Chapple, A.R. Coulter, Reg Counsell, Mrs D.M. Crabtree, Vi Crook, Mrs K. Dodkin, Don Earl, Mrs Olwen Evans, M. Free, John Furbank, Mrs P. Gamby, Geoffrey Garbutt, Mrs M.C. Gardner, Fred Goldman, Barry Goldsmith, Bert Gooch, Dennis Green, Jean Grierson, Lynford R. Hampton, Mrs E. Harvey, John Hayes, G. Hoar, Mrs D. Hudson, Mrs M. Kearsley, Mrs J. Kipling, James Kirk, Eileen Landalls, Mrs Peggy Lawson, Mark Leopold, Mary Lines, R.V. Lloyd, Joy Long, R. McDonnell, Mrs P. McGuigan, P.L. McKiernan, Kevin McWilliam, Jilly Maynard, Bert Millgate, B. Moxain, Sylvia Olney, Mrs A.C. Pickett, Sheila Pringle, H.G.W. Prytherch, Jessie Pym, Mrs M. Richardson, Terry Rolt, Maurice Rooney, George Rosie, Edwin Sippel, Harold Smith, Bernard Spencer, Roy Stevens, D.E. Taylor, Patricia Tester, Meg Thomas, Mrs P. Thomas, Shirley Thomas, Mrs Celia Tripp, Adrian Uribe, Jill Walden, Mollie Warner, Margaret Whiting, Tom Winzor, Winifred Wood, B. Woollacott, Mrs Geraldine Zappella.

Some contributors preferred that their comments remain anonymous. Therefore, not all quotes in the text are credited.

The poem 'Drinking Bitters' and the cartoon on pp. 51 and 16 are reprinted with permission from *European and Pacific Stars and Stripes*. The photographs of Clark Gable on pp. 53 and 57 by permission of Michael Downes.

My husband has, as always, cheerfully and enthusiastically helped me at every stage of the book.

Touching up the artwork on a B-24 at Sudbury, c. 1944. (US Air Force Academy)

CHAPTER I

Prelude

It is common knowledge that during the 1930s the United States of America was overwhelmingly isolationist. Not for a second time would they come to the rescue of a tottering French Republic and an imperialistic British Empire. To emphasise that fact Congress had passed the Neutrality Act in August 1935, the policy of which was to have no foreign policy. President Franklin Delano Roosevelt was well aware of the dangers threatened by the fascist powers but, until his renomination for a third term in November 1940, he had to toe a very fine line to appease both Congress and the isolationists. 'Your boys', he said in an election speech, 'are not going to be sent to any foreign wars.' When Hitler's troops marched into Poland on 1 September 1939 the USA was doing a great deal of business with Germany, and a considerable number of American citizens were of German origin. Luckily, many were also of British origin, and they set out to support the motherland. The British War Relief Society came into being as war was declared and in very short time it was highly organised, staffed entirely by volunteers. The British government paid the carriage on the hundreds of thousands of very welcome 'Bundles for Britain' which were shipped to the British Isles throughout the war. The society also financed the more than a thousand Queen's Messengers, the mobile kitchens that operated in blitzed cities and, perhaps best of all, ran British Merchant Navy clubs at twenty-seven ports along the eastern seaboard, which fed, clothed and fêted the men who had lost everything through enemy action. Astonishing sums of money were collected from those sympathetic Americans who also funded the American Hospital in London.

As war began Roosevelt appointed Gen George C. Marshall his Chief of Staff, a man of authority and integrity who fought hard to get the American military prepared for what both he and Roosevelt feared was to come, though always hoping to avoid it. During 1940 and 1941 Marshall pressed constantly for an increased armed forces budget, while Roosevelt sent his personal envoys to London on fact-finding missions. He did not trust the views expressed by his ambassador Joseph P. Kennedy, who was from the outset convinced that the British were going to be beaten, as was the America First Party – with its star member the ace pilot Charles Lindbergh – formed in 1940 by those equally convinced that Germany was the horse to put money on. After Dunkirk American preparedness moved into a higher gear, Marshall sought a regular army of 750,000 by the end of 1941 and a vast expansion of the aircraft-building programme. After the fall of France Roosevelt, even more anxious to help supply Britain without compromising the Neutrality Act, arranged for 500,000 ex-First World War rifles considered 'surplus' to be shipped across. Col Henry Stimson, Secretary for War, was Marshall's ally in Congress and between them they managed to push through, as German bombs rained on London in the September of 1940, the Selective Service Act, the more acceptable name for conscription.

Britain by this time was broke, and the life-saving Lend-Lease Act, giving her credit up to 7 billion dollars, was passed in March 1941. Eventually, Winston Churchill got his fifty warships, the USA got her bases in the Caribbean and RAF aircrew were trained in the sunny southern states of the USA. Stanley Freestone was one of them, arriving in Georgia in July 1941. He was trained entirely by American personnel, civil and military, and in the West Point tradition to a very high standard. To preserve the letter of American neutrality the RAF cadets wore civilian clothes off base. At the same time Allied warships were being repaired in American ports and, most importantly, joint British and American staff talks planned grand strategy on a basis of probability. In January 1941 President Roosevelt sent his own man, Harry Hopkins, to London to assess the situation. There he met Gen Raymond E. Lee, American military attaché, confirmed Anglophile, 'to Hell with Hitler, I say', and a man with contacts in high places. Lee was delighted when Joseph Kennedy was replaced by John G. Winant, a totally different kettle of fish. Lee comments on the endless stream of FDR's personal representatives, military missions and fact-finding missions that were beginning to swamp Grosvenor Square during 1941. The brief of one Special Observer Group was to pinpoint suitable sites for American bases should the worst happen. Construction of air bases actually began in June 1941 using local labour and 350 American 'technical advisors'. After the German invasion of Russia Hopkins – dubbed by Churchill 'Lord Root of the Matter' – was again sent to London, and this time on to Russia to assess Russian needs. The USA's official neutrality was wearing distinctly thin.

It was becoming even more obvious where the President's sympathies lay when he and Churchill met in August 1941 aboard the USS *Augusta* in Placentia Bay, Newfoundland. Churchill had travelled over on HMS *Prince of Wales* at some risk. The Atlantic Charter that they jointly declared was not really of particular significance at the time; what really mattered was Roosevelt's firm commitment to the war against Germany and the friendship that deepened between the two leaders. Almost to the day the extension to the Selective Service Act had scraped through the House of Representatives by one solitary vote; a maximum of 900,000 men could now be drafted annually for a 1-year period.

However, the USA was well represented on the fighting front long before Pearl Harbor. Probably as many as 10,000 Americans had crossed the border into Canada to join up, some were recruited, financed and shipped through Canada to Britain by a Col Charles Sweeney. The London end of this operation was taken care of by his nephews Charles (first husband of Margaret, Duchess of Argyll) and Robert. The Sweeneys knew all the right people, and the Air Council was persuaded to agree to the formation of an American squadron within the Royal Air Force. The first group sailed in August 1940, and No. 71 Sqn was formed at Church Fenton in Yorkshire. The second, No. 121, was assembled in May 1941 and the third, No. 133, followed in August. They lived on RAF stations, were paid as RAF aircrew, ate British rations and flew Spitfires that were serviced by RAF ground crew. These Americans who flew with what came to be known as the Eagle Squadrons were often qualified civil pilots who did not meet United States Army Air Force (USAAF) requirements for one reason or another; they certainly didn't do it for the money. Nor were they military men: as one RAF officer put it, 'They were noisy, they forgot military courtesy, they had horrible table manners and drinking habits. They were in the true sense civilians for whom military courtesy and discipline had no meaning.' The British public saw them differently: they were heroes who had come to help, nothing was too good for them and many a landlord passed over a free beer. The Eagle boys were by no means the only Americans serving in the RAF. Robert Raymond, no youngster at twenty-eight, working at his father's furniture store in Kansas City gave 'restlessness' as his reason for joining the American Volunteer Ambulance Corps in France. When the French surrendered, he found his own way to Lisbon and thence back to Britain where he joined the RAF and got his aircrew training in Canada. He served in Bomber Command, not transferring to USAAF until July 1943. Less known is the fact that there were Americans serving in the Royal Navy and as ground crew in the RAF.

In every respect 1941 was the crunch year. The threat of a German invasion of the British Isles had receded dramatically when in June Hitler launched Barbarossa, the invasion of Russia. American troops replaced the British troops who had occupied Iceland when Denmark was overrun and, following the attack by a German submarine on the American destroyer *Greer*, the US Navy extended its patrol into the Atlantic. No lives were lost on that occasion but other ships were attacked, and late in October another destroyer, *Reuben James*, was torpedoed with heavy casualties. Congress agreed to the arming of merchant ships and other amendments to the Neutrality Act even as the rumblings from the Far East grew louder.

The still somewhat minimal American armed forces were already stretched to maximum extension garrisoning the Philippines and Hawaiian Islands, as well as the continental USA. In 1940 Japan had formed an alliance with Germany and Italy and during 1941 several other events took place which rang alarm bells. There was a change of government in Japan, which brought in the militaristic Gen Tojo, first as Minister of War then in September as Prime Minister. The USA imposed economic sanctions on Japan and froze all her assets as the Vichy French government granted Japan the use of airfields and bases in what was then French Indo-China. London was passing on intelligence reports of Japan's aggressive intentions, and the Americans themselves had broken Japanese diplomatic codes. Gen Marshall continued to reinforce Gen MacArthur in the Philippines and upgrade defences of the Hawaiian Islands. Roosevelt was still trying to secure a diplomatic settlement of the difficulties in the Far East when Pearl Harbor was attacked on 7 December 1941.

All hell broke loose as the Japanese struck at both British and American bases in the Pacific and South China Sea; there were no more choices. The Hearst press and Lindbergh's America First Committee did a quick *volte-face* and rallied behind their President. Volunteers flooded the recruiting offices and local draft boards were granted yet further powers. The Army as usual was the poor relation as volunteers flocked to the Navy and Air Force. Minimum height for the Navy was 5 ft 2 in, for the Army a mere 5 ft. At first only single men were drafted, but by the end of the war everybody was taken, including men wearing glasses – even men with only one eye – illiterates and felons. But, the Government Issue, the GI, who was about to flood the continent of Europe was, as Les Kennett puts it, a member of 'the best fed, best dressed, best equipped army in the world'.

CHAPTER 2
First Impressions

Although the Japanese caught the US Navy and Army napping at Pearl Harbor, the framework was in place in the European Theatre of Operations (ETO). It had already been decided that the Germans had to be defeated by a land invasion for which Britain was the ideal base. It possessed the necessary infrastructure, a highly developed industry, railway network, communications and existing airfields and military installations. Other airfields, specifically for American occupation, had been under construction since June 1941, particularly in Northern Ireland, where 5 camps for 1,000 men apiece were already in preparation. Londoners, especially around the West End, were already familiar with the accent humming around Grosvenor Square (later to be termed 'Eisenhowerplatz').

The first troops to arrive on this side of the Atlantic were units of the 34th Division, codename Magnet (the transportation of American troops to

Preparing to receive our Allies, Londonderry. (Imperial War Museum A9593)

Pte Milburn Henke officially first ashore at Dufferin Quay, Belfast, 26 January 1942. (IWM H16847)

Northern Ireland). On 26 January 1942 4,000 men, including Maj-Gens Chaney and Hartle, arrived and, as they disembarked at Dufferin Quay in Belfast, the band of the Royal Ulster Rifles played the 'Star Spangled Banner'. One soldier, Pte M.H. Henke, was celebrated as the first GI ashore, though in fact other units had disembarked earlier. The men wore the First World War type helmet to avoid alarming the local population, since the up-to-date version resembled that worn by the German Army. What first struck the inhabitants of Belfast was the lack of noise. Accustomed as they were to the clattering of boots on concrete when British soldiers passed by, the movement of the Americans was like a phantom army in their rubber-soled boots. Even small children noticed that they were not too concerned with discipline and tended to slouch about, in marked contrast to the British soldiers. The children were quick enough to latch on to the benefits, however, as showers of candy and gum came their way.

But what were they thinking, these men of the 34th, and the hundreds of thousands who were to follow? Most of them did not want to come and, even after the attack on Pearl Harbor, considered that the war in Europe was none of their business. They wanted to get it over with as quickly as possible. The United States of America was not an ethnic entity; there was thus the natural antagonism of those of Irish antecedents towards the British, that of the Italians whom the British were fighting in North Africa, and of course the Germans, unless they were refugees from the current regime. One of the latter, aged nineteen, already in the Army, was given American nationality at a special court hearing so that he could fight with his unit in Europe. Many other servicemen, probably the bulk from 'middle America', had been influenced by the isolationism of the Republican and America First parties; the British were being overwhelmed by Rommel and 'couldn't fight their way out of a paper bag'. Many of these same men were to be horrified by the bomb damage at the ports of entry, and put into a panic when they first heard an air-raid warning siren.

The United States Navy arrives at Londonderry, January 1942. (IWM HU54538)

Nor was the journey across the Atlantic in British ships conducive to good relations with their allies. Jules Honig, with the 4th Division, came over on the *Princess of Bedford*, a banana boat built to carry a maximum of 80 passengers, but now carrying 250 soldiers:

> Some slept on tables in the mess hall, others on deck where they were regularly drenched with cold, salt water. There were only two meals daily and the continuous meal line stretched several lengths of the ship. The morning meal was oatmeal, tea and powdered eggs (green). The main meal consisted of rice, lemonade and a greasy hunk of liver . . . once we got our slop many of us would toss it overboard. Almost everybody got sea sick and many also had diarrhoea. The stench from that combination was overbearing, especially below deck. The madness lasted 17 days and nights. What a sight we must have presented as we dragged down that gang plank (at Greenock) with our duffel bags and smelling of puke and excrement.

Other GIs have the same recollections of 'filthy' British ships, where GIs were sold extra food at black-market prices, or tried to gulp down the 'swill' they were served. One luckless passenger lost 25 lbs in fourteen days. Even the more fortunate who came across on one of the big ships – the Queens could do it in under five days – were subject to overcrowding and bad food. A state room intended for one loving couple now accommodated nine men, five up one wall and four down the other. The food served aboard British ships pleased nobody, although the officers fared better later in the war. HMS *Diadem* gave a lift home to some twenty American sailors who had delivered an American warship to the Russians. Bert Millgate, a RN rating, remembers that when given the same food as the ship's company the 'gobs' threw it overboard. They were then served officers' rations.

American servicemen never did take to the British diet, apart from fish and chips: they all seem most to recall greasy mutton and brussels sprouts. (One notable exception, Marion Free, stationed in Kent with the 9th Air Force, 'loved brussels sprouts' and still has them.) Given meat pies on arrival most GIs discarded them, doubtless to the horror of the nice middle-aged English ladies who were handing them out, 'no taste' and undefinable filling. British-style sausages caused a shudder, tasted like sawdust and brought home to one soldier just how bad things were in Britain. Another GI could never reconcile the fact that British Army kitchens were so filthy, considering so much emphasis was put on 'spit and polish'. The less-than-white wartime loaf of bread was either loathed or loved and tea was eventually grudgingly accepted since it was better than the alternative attempt to produce coffee. In fact, GIs working alongside British servicemen quite took to the 4 o'clock tea break. The pamphlet 'Instructions for American Servicemen in Britain 1942' put it rather well: 'The British don't know how to make a good cup of coffee. You don't know how to make a good cup of tea. It's an even swap.'

The American servicemen's very own newspaper, the *Stars and Stripes*, reported in November 1943 that the NAAFI were making an effort to serve American-style coffee, and attempting to make hamburgers. So distasteful was the British service diet that was served initially to all GIs that the hierarchy was soon forced to use precious shipping space to import American food – peanut butter, Coca-Cola, white flour, canned fruits and juices – to quell possible riots. It worked the other way too. A Merchant Navy man who found himself temporarily in Hartford, Connecticut, hoped he would not have to eat 'ghastly' American food such as candied sweet potatoes, tea with tea bags and cold beer. There are innumerable food stories, including the famous one, possibly apocryphal, attributed to Col Stanley Wray of the 91st Bomb Group, to the effect that if one of his pilots had to ditch would they please make sure it was on a field of brussels sprouts. John Hayes, then aged twelve, remembers his sister inviting a Yank boyfriend to share a meal with the family. The meal was bubble and squeak, John obligingly explained what it was, and was then able to 'scoff the lot' himself. Needless to say, the GI thought they were starving and arrived a couple of nights later with enough 'tinned food to feed us for a month'.

Once the men arrived at their port of entry – Belfast, Greenock or Liverpool – they usually entrained for the next stage of their mystery tour, although by now they at least knew it was Britain. Some were quite taken with the smaller British train, though few went as far as a soldier of the 101st Airborne, who said he thought British trains superior and American railroads could 'learn a thing or two'. He thought compartments not a bad idea, easy to use for boarding and exiting and avoided jammed aisles, while giving privacy to small groups. Others thought the trains small and noisy, 'reminded me of a bedtime children's book *The Little Engine that Could*', and were scathing of the tiny trains that stopped seemingly every 5 minutes. Even worse, if there was no corridor there were no lavatories. But John Costello was enchanted: 'Oh to be on an English train rolling through the countryside between Liverpool and Tidworth; standing in the aisle seeing all those thin, neat, closely packed victory gardens. To get up and stretch your legs, then pause and see out of a window, and having six or seven companions alongside to converse with.' Later GIs came to appreciate the intimacy a non-corridor train afforded, particularly if a pretty girl was in the same carriage.

'Sure is cosier than the trains back home.' (IWM EA18101)

On his journey from Greenock to Suffolk Robert Arbib, a sergeant with the Aviation Battalion the 820th Engineers and an early arrival, was instantly smitten with the 'incredibly green and trim landscape'. Arbib, a resounding Anglophile, always found it a 'joy to walk through the Suffolk countryside'. This sentiment was frequently expressed, 'breathtakingly beautiful'. Many GIs were simply over-whelmed by the sheer verdancy of the English countryside, the lack of billboards, the postcard-pretty villages with thatched cottages and hedgerows. Everything confirmed that vision of England that had been conjured up by the movies, probably *Mrs Miniver*, the Greer Garson and Walter Pidgeon tearjerker. One southern Californian was enchanted by the proliferation of flowers and the hanging baskets outside pubs, much preferring it to the arid deserts of his homeland. To quote an airman from the 91st Bomb Group, 'we'll think of England in the spring, the clean fresh smell of the soil, the daffodils, the apple blossom, the song birds, the rain, the long summer days and the English roses'.

All was not sunshine and flowers, however, on that first train ride. Men travelling south from Glasgow through the Gorbals, then one of the worst slum areas in the British Isles, were struck by the shabbily dressed children begging along the track. Glasgow in the 1940s was an unlovely place, battered, 'soot streaked' and, rather like coming into London via Liverpool Street station, gave the very worst impression. Then, too, many boarded their first train in the black-out, into unventilated, probably unheated, barely lit carriages and passed through bomb-damaged cities like Liverpool, where fog-shrouded shells of buildings loomed out of the darkness. Wartime train journeys, though frequently very social, were never comfortable, always overcrowded, corridors jammed with bodies and kitbags and choking with cigarette smoke.

Naturally the narrow winding roads caused plenty of comment, as did the small cars. The official little green book pointed out that British automobiles were little and low powered because all the gasoline (petrol) had to be imported. The twists and turns of the country lanes were to prove a nightmare for the drivers of the large American trucks and 40-ft loaders, and even more so while driving on the 'wrong' side of the road. An added hazard was the lack of road signs, all having been removed in 1940, and motoring GIs were frequently and significantly lost. There were many accidents, particularly in the black-out, and many corner buildings had lumps sheared off. Some took better care: 'we always had to make

The American Red Cross ladies are everywhere. (IWM H37401)

sure the trucks could turn without hitting the houses, sometimes we had to jockey a corner in order to carry on; also had to watch the road for cyclists'. Cyclists were another problem: a rarity on American roads, in Britain the bicycle was probably the commonest mode of transport. In the black-out, barely lit, they were an additional hazard for the unwary GI driver, often whipping along at excessive speeds. Somewhat ironically there were even more accidents when GIs took to this two-wheeled mode of transport.

That was in the locality of the camp. When it came to going further afield GIs quickly got the hang of the available transport, piling onto buses, into trains and, in London, the Underground. They even got accustomed to queuing for everything. One was impressed by the London Underground, which compared favourably with the New York subway, 'Modern trains, escalators, better lighting and very clean.' Another was very taken with the ingenious gas tanks that replaced petrol on some buses, which sometimes had to offload passengers when taking a hill, but 'no one ever complained'. The black-out was a shock to all the Americans and it took time to become accustomed to it, 'several times we went into ditches alongside the road; I finally rigged a flashlight that would only shine downwards'.

Another pitfall for the new arrival was the English currency. Arbib again: 'he ridicules the monetary system the first time he changes a pound note . . . the pounds, shillings and pence, and above all the apparently superfluous guinea,

The 355th Fighter Group march into Steeple Morden, July 1943. (Ken Wells)

seem unnecessarily and aggravatingly complex, and he solves the matter by offering a note in payment for every purchase, accepting the change without question. But, after his first poker game, when he must make lightning and intricate transactions with the coins, he has no more trouble.' The same went for the men the first time they hit town and crowded into a pub. Most GIs simply proffered a note, accepting whatever change was given, puzzling over the assorted, illogical coinage and severely taxing the patience of the landlord. For those soldiers only in Britain on a short-term basis for the D-Day build-up the currency often remained a problem. Easier for them the decimal systems of continental Europe.

What of the GIs' first encounters with the native population? There were some less than happy experiences on the journey across but others were different again: 'my first encounter

Finding the way around the village of Litlington. (Ken Wells)

with a Englishman was when I asked him the name of the ship, he was most helpful. All in all he spoke with all the men in the stateroom, advising what to do about seasickness etc.' This particular 9th Air Force man always found people 'helpful', being a quietly spoken polite man himself, but it is reiterated by many others. 'Taxi drivers know their job and are courteous and helpful' (apart from those who regularly ripped off the Americans). British policemen, the bobbies, were popular, happy to give directions and always ended any exchange with 'You can't miss it'. Arbib is particularly admiring of the village constable who, with no weapon except a quiet dignity and a sense of authority, was respected by locals and GIs alike, and smoothed relations between the two factions. Since it had been agreed that the American military police (nicknamed 'Snowdrops' because of their white helmets) would have sole jurisdiction over American servicemen, the British policeman did remain a benign figure to most GIs. A visiting sailor always found the British far more amiable (than his compatriots) to strangers in shops and on trains and buses. GIs were especially fascinated by bus conductresses, and delighted in the exchange of banter in which these ladies excelled as they goodnaturedly grappled with the wartime overload of passengers. (One comments he was always afraid the double-deckers would overturn going round

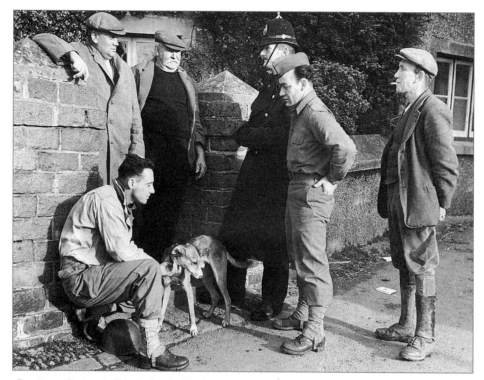

Getting acquainted with the locals. (IWM EA34045)

corners.) They equally admired the female railway porters and bus drivers, and were particularly partial to Land Girls and British servicewomen. Since there was no conscription of women in the USA – a fact their government came to regret – girls in uniform were a novelty and enthusiastically courted.

'Women; Ah there's the rub,' says Lynford Hampton, 'during wartime this situation is magnified.' The 'here today, gone tomorrow' and even 'tomorrow may never come' philosophy is very much heightened in wartime. Everybody wanted a good time and 'beer and broads' was usually the answer. Girls were pursued with enthusiasm by the majority of these young men away from home. There were plenty of shy GIs, and plenty inhibited by their religious and moral upbringing, but they melted into the background. Mostly they whistled and yelled at anything in a skirt as one British girl recalls, 'every time an American truck passed me on my bike I could guarantee being loudly appreciated; mind you the same applied to British soldiers'. GIs mostly went for the local girls in a big way: 'I just love the way you talk'. There were as many types of girls as there were of GIs and probably some of each weren't too fussy but, overall, nice men were attracted to nice girls, who delighted in the attention showered upon them. There were, of course, Americans who had nothing good to say about English girls, even when they used them. They were scathing of bad teeth, body odour, their lack of sophistication and shabby clothes. All the GIs were puzzled by the red-marked shins of British women, the result of sitting in front of coal fires.

Though many Americans appreciated the beauty of an English springtime, what they remember most is the rain and fog. When coal fires were the prime source of heat, thick fog was a commonplace in the winter months. To be in a London 'pea-souper' was an unforgettable experience; it was difficult to breathe and impossible to see anything even in daylight. In the black-out it was like moving through a thick curtain: 'I remember crawling along at about a mile an hour, my passenger, head out of the window, directing my every inch.' Soot-laden fog coated everything, a day in London inevitably produced dirty hands, faces, hair and clothing. The rural fogs were less yellow but equally hazardous to traffic, the GI drivers had never seen the like. Flying missions were frequently cancelled because of fog, low cloud base or poor visibility. Then there was the seemingly incessant rain which intensified the damp and cold and added to the general discomfort of the Nissen hut, 'an ice-box open at both ends', where it was almost impossible to dry wet clothes and always smelt damp. Contrary to general belief, it did not rain all the time. In East Anglia, home to most of the air bases, rainfall was actually below average. It did, however, drizzle little and often, and the winter skies tended to be gloomy more often than not.

Home from home in a Nissen hut at Steeple Morden. (Ken Wells)

Added to the grey skies was, alas, the grey of the landscape and population after three years of war. No materials were available for house maintenance and only bomb damage qualified a householder to claim scarce building supplies and labour, the private house was at the bottom of the pile in a war economy. In public parks flower displays were replaced by cabbage patches, lawns stayed uncut and hedges untrimmed. Most homes and businesses had strips of brown paper stuck over windows to minimise blast damage. On the high street, shop fronts were sadly in need of a lick of paint and broken windows were boarded up. The shops themselves were understocked and understaffed, unbelievably closed over lunchtimes and one afternoon a week was dubbed 'early closing'. Air-raid shelters, of which there were several types, all ugly, did not contribute to the aesthetic appearance of any street, neither did the emergency water tanks for fire fighters, nor the sandbags piled around municipal buildings. Most people, apart from those in uniform, looked drab of necessity. Dark clothes showed the

" What's cooking, brother ? Storin' mud for next winter ? "

A cartoon featured in the Stars and Stripes. (With permission from *European and Pacific Stars and Stripes*)

dirt less and rationing kept replacements to a minimum. Lucky was the woman who had managed to get hold of some parachute silk. As the little book said, 'If British civilians look dowdy or badly dressed it is not because they do not like good clothes or know how to wear them. All clothing is rationed and the British know that they help war production by wearing an old suit or dress.' So little boys wore short trousers made out of a grandmother's skirt and girls made skirts from old curtains. Small wonder so many GIs dubbed the British Isles dingy, dull and shabby. 'The rare occasions that we were able to move off base left a stark impression. There were bombed-out houses in all towns and villages', Jules Honig recalls, 'and a harried-looking populace in ragged clothing moved about.'

To most GIs Britain remained a small, backward country and they found it difficult to credit the British with anything much, 'They absolutely refused to believe we had had television before the war', says Betty Kieffer. John Colville, Churchill's private secretary, tells a lovely story of an American Liberator pilot returning to the USA after an operational tour, and therefore no stranger to Britain, aboard the *Queen Mary*. He told Colville how much he had enjoyed his stay and thought it right that the American government should have named such a magnificent ship after an English queen. The pilot took some convincing that the 'biggest ships in the world' could not be American. While it is true that many GIs were fascinated by the storybook castles, one woman will never forget showing an American around Windsor Castle. His only comment was 'It's all so old, and what about the plumbing?'

When GIs began to experience local hospitality they were to discover how the British lived. Not the hospitality of the grand houses, for this was for selected groups only, but the hospitality of the man from the pub, the nearby farmer, the local bobby, a girlfriend's family. The semi-detached three-up, two-down or terraced house was a particularly British phenomenon. 'I was always impressed by the smallness of things in England, the small size of hallways and rooms.' Of his future in-laws' house, a typical such semi, Stan Kieffer writes, 'Two adults, three girls lived in the house, and there was always room for three, four or five GIs, rather like a beehive, but always great good feelings, and we never felt rejected.' This house had indoor plumbing while many did not, especially in rural areas. One lady living near Aldermaston still recalls the night an officer 'in his fancy pink pants fell into a ditch looking for our privy bucket. But the Americans always accepted us as we were.' They were not so happy about the British-style shiny, non-absorbent toilet paper though; one GI kept his fiancée's family supplied with this commodity, American-style (literally Government Issue), and later sent packages of it over from France. American servicemen were apparently allowed some twenty-two pieces daily, as opposed to the four pieces allotted British servicemen, a very significant example of Uncle Sam's horn of plenty. Gradually, the Americans became accustomed to the strange but familiar language, 'words which first startled and amused us': petrol, queue, torch, tuppence ha'penny, bloody, spanner, prang, 'you've had it', 'pull the chain'; as did the English to the vagaries of the American vocabulary.

If they were in the country long enough, most Americans accepted the bad along with the good, the endless dark winter nights in the black-out contrasting with the beauty and long days of early summer; the shabbiness of London, but at the same time the incredible conviviality of wartime Britain.

Speaking of black-outs, you know how dark it can get in Cambridge when there is no moon. One such night a certain Major had gone into Cambridge with the motor pool ace, Pte. Rape, as his driver. When it came time to go home he couldn't find Rape so he started shouting in the middle of the square 'Rape, Rape'. You can imagine the response he got. Then the Luftwaffe attacks on London in the early days of 1944, when we used to stand out at night and watch the searchlights, the pyrotechnics of the ack-ack defence, the glow of London burning. We won't forget that last train back with all those touching little platform scenes as the Joes kissed the gals goodbye and staggered aboard. And when the local finally reached Royston there was always some joker who opened the door on the wrong side and stepped off into black space to land in a heap on the rail track.

In the many interviews and reminiscences recorded since those war years one comment overrides all others and that is the way they, the GIs, were treated by the British people they got to know personally. A letter in the *Stars and Stripes* of November 1944 from H.J. Nunes, a GI who had been billeted in private homes sums it up: 'I can truthfully say that the hospitality and kindness that was shown to me will equal any I have received anywhere . . . furthermore they made me feel at home. The trust they placed in me shall never be forgotten and I sure appreciated everything they did for me.'

CHAPTER 3
Impact

It was undoubtedly the children who were unstintingly bowled over by the Yanks. The very first GI who gave a child a piece of candy or gum was responsible for whatever followed. Every child at the time, however young, remembers that munificence above all. Jilly Maynard remembers: 'It was 1944 and my mother and I were standing on the platform at Devizes waiting for our train. I was nearly four. As we waited a troop train passed through the station, not stopping but going very slowly. The open windows were crammed with faces but as one window passed me a voice shouted "Hi Ginge". The voice came from a young man with fair hair who leant out of the window and threw at my feet a shower of chewing gum. I looked up and our eyes met. I'm sure I would recognise him today! I had never had any sweets or chocolate, and to me it was the most marvellous gift I ever received.' The word spread like wildfire; the children holding their hands

Three sisters are entertained at an American Mess. Betty Kieffer is on the right. (Betty Kieffer)

out in the Gorbals and the small boys forever chasing American trucks in the hope of a 'drop'. An older Cambridgeshire schoolgirl recalls locally stationed GIs bringing trays of sweets to the school for everybody to share: 'Sometimes they would come over with drinking chocolate, and we would take an empty tin to school so we could bring the chocolate home. Sometimes they would throw you an orange.' At the wonderful children's parties there might be a banana on every child's plate. Most small children had never even seen a banana, they had no idea that it had to be peeled first. Given a ride in a jeep and taken to the mess hall for a meal, one fourteen-year-old never forgot the plate upon which everything was heaped, meat, potatoes, dessert, the lot. She started to eat what she thought were mashed potatoes, scoop-shaped as her mother served them, and found it to be whipped butter. Probably a week's ration for four, and even today, she is still not fond of butter. Her nine-year-old sister said 'this Mess really is a mess'.

It was not only the candy, gum and parties. Many children separated from their parents found affection as well as generosity. One unhappy girl evacuated to Yeovil recalls, 'it was the worst time of my life, and I thought my parents didn't want me any more. I shall always be thankful to those Americans, for they saved us and made our time as evacuees more bearable. Every evening after school, and a sparse tea, we would make a beeline for the camp, where we were really spoilt. I remember Tootsie rolls, sponge cakes with loads of cream and always plenty of doughnuts and oranges, and American comics by the armful.' Significantly she adds, 'Grown ups, that was obvious, weren't keen on the Americans, but to us they were the Best. They told us stories and spoke of home, and one American would strum a guitar and sing songs with tears on his cheeks. As each group left it was like party time, they emptied their pockets of money and left boxes of oranges at the gate.'

For children during the war the parties thrown by GIs all over the country were something they would always remember. Not just the shower of sweets, cakes, ice-cream and exotic fizzy drinks, but the warmth and easy-going friendliness of their hosts. The *Stars and Stripes* reported a Thanksgiving party for 200 orphans in 1942. The newspaper itself raised a fund for British orphans, a large number of whom had actually lost parents as a result of enemy bombing. One GI gave £20, his month's pay. The servicemen were horrified by the considerable bomb damage they saw in the big cities, the shabby clothes and pale faces of the inhabitants and, because of the rationing of food on a scale unimagined in the USA, thought the British were starving. To feed and spoil the children was the obvious and uncomplicated way to help these vulnerable

GIs in the London area with some of the 650 orphans they took to see the film My Friend Flicka *with supper afterwards.* (IWM AP1866)

members of society, as it helped those men homesick for their own children. Almost every station would organise a Christmas party. The 8th Air Force groups in the area threw a party for 500 children on Christmas Eve 1943 in the Royston cinema. At Bovingdon there was an added attraction for the children, who were shown over a B-17 Flying Fortress. Many of the men spent their off-duty hours making toys in the base workshops, or asked families back home to send gifts for the children for, by the time the bulk of the American forces arrived in Britain, toys were virtually unobtainable in the shops.

For those small boys living close to an airfield or camp it was a magical time. For many of them, hungering to be RAF fighter pilots, it nurtured a lifelong fascination. They spent all their free time, and probably a lot that wasn't, hanging around their mentors, even inside security areas. Grammar schoolboy Joe Duggan, evacuated to Buckfastleigh in Devon, hit the jackpot. He was billeted with a tolerant young woman with a small baby, whose husband was away in the 8th Army. They lived in a flat in an old disused mill, the mill itself being occupied by a succession of British Army units. Then his life changed.

Dancing with the little girls. (IWM EA6859)

One afternoon (in about Christmas 1943) the whole village was swarming with American troops and vehicles – Battery B of the 459th Battalion of the 29th Division had arrived! They had about ten four-wheeled anti-aircraft guns (we called them Bofors) towed by trucks. Battery B was commanded by a Captain Weston, his jeep was called *Bouncing Bitch* but most others had more refined names such as *Betty Grable.* The soldiers were surprised to find that I, too, lived at the mill, and sweet rationing was over for me, as I had a constant supply of chocolate bars and chewing gum. I spent every free moment with my Yanks – all members of the same gun crew – I don't think there were many 13 year olds who played with a real Tommy gun. When a strict top sergeant saw me on a bunk the first time and asked what I was doing there, the soldiers replied 'He lives here!'.

Another child who never forgot the GIs was the ten-year-old Harold Smith who lived in Swansea opposite a hotel much frequented by the Americans. One day he

Lt Henry Brown, top ace of the 355th, with a young visitor at Steeple Morden. (Ken Wells)

A helping hand at Steeple Morden. (Ken Wells)

A young Basil Taylor with Earl Mock, who found him again after a 56-year interval. (Ken Wells)

The 355th entertain local children, Christmas 1944. (Ken Wells)

was knocked down by a car after chasing a ball into the road and critically injured. An American soldier gave him crucial first aid which probably saved his life.

Schoolteachers were less enchanted by the preoccupation with gum chewing and one lad was most upset when his teacher would not let a group of visiting GIs talk to the children because they were chewing gum and setting a bad example. Another enthusiastic gum chewer Barry Goldsmith, then seven years old, whose house backed onto a school being used both as a transit camp and for men working on the docks, remembers that his family befriended many of the men including one of the camp cooks. This GI kept them supplied with all manner of unheard-of treats, such as orange juice, lemon meringue pie and, most exciting of all, gave him his very first Coca-Cola. 'Along with other boys in the street I spent a lot of time chatting to the American M.P.s at the gate of the school. They were more relaxed and tolerant than the British and would let us sit in the sentry box. Every evening a jeep would arrive from the American bakery about a mile away in Swaythling. There would always be a tray of doughnuts for us boys, at least one for each of us, two if we were lucky.'

When the Americans took over Brock Barracks in Reading, literally at the bottom of David Brinsden's garden, he, along with the other neighbourhood children, spent as much time as he could visiting the GIs in their huts. One of his jobs was to go to the fish and chip shop to buy supper for which he was given a 10*s* note and allowed to keep the change, a considerable sum. Sometimes he and his mother were awakened late at night by GIs climbing over the high fence at the side of their house in order to sneak back into barracks unnoticed. 'The GIs at all times treated us children with kindness and consideration, one question they all asked was did we have any older sisters.' A thirteen-year-old girl in Swansea was fortunate enough to have two soldiers billeted with her family for the D-Day build-up. They collected her from school in a jeep, to the envy of the other girls, treated the family to outings and taught her to jitterbug; more tearful farewells. Billeting was not always an unmitigated success. Although the children of one family adored their lodger for the usual reasons, their father was furious when a cherished bottle of whisky disappeared in his absence.

Roy Stevens sums up the American experience from the schoolboy's point of view. In 1942, aged eight, he was living in the Dorset village of Broadstone, which had already experienced incursions by Canadian, French and Moroccan troops.

But the Yanks were something else entirely. They exuded an air of sophistication mixed with a certain degree of charming naiveté which completely bowled us over. For a start their uniforms were well cut and they wore brown boots with rubber soles and heels. They smoked cigars and seemed to have money to burn. All this, together with their exotic accents was a devastating blend, especially to the local girls. The American forces requisitioned several large properties in the village, and the Broadstone Golf Club became their Officers' Mess. I remember we boys used to rummage in the kitchen trash cans, and would sometimes come up with such treasures as cans of orange juice or spaghetti. An empty shop in the village was taken over as the PX store, and once a week the GIs drew their rations of cigarettes, candy and gum. On the appointed day we boys would lay siege to the store and waylay the emerging goodie-laden Yanks with cries of 'Any gum chum'. The soldiers, understandably, soon got tired of this, and hit on a particularly ingenious idea. Each soldier adopted one of us boys and only gave out candy to his particular chosen one. At Christmas time the Yanks laid on a slap-up party in the Women's Institute. Afterwards we were given rides in their jeeps. I hung on for dear life as our driver careered around the streets of

Broadstone at breakneck speed. As D-Day approached the Americans began to leave the village, I remember seeing off my Top Sergeant 'Uncle' from Texas with a large lump in my throat. Did he survive? I shall never know. It's true to say, that for a brief period, our lives had been transformed by those big-hearted GIs from across the Pond. Things would never be quite the same again.

This last sentiment was echoed by many more of those, children at the time, who had delighted in the warmth, kindness and generosity shown them by these homesick young men.

The GIs made an equally strong impression on the female population. Who could resist the cheery 'Hiya Babe' or 'Hiya Honey' from these smiling, well-dressed, presentable young men, displaying their own even white teeth? 'A breath of fresh air', 'Just like a movie star'. They walked differently, tending to adopt a relaxed stroll, unlike the boot-dominated rigidity of our own servicemen. Their uniforms were so smooth and well fitting that many privates were initially taken for officers. The *Cambridge Daily News* published on 31 August 1942 a 'Guide to American

Making friends, Weston Hills, Baldock. (Ken Wells)

Uniforms'. After relating stories about British servicemen saluting American
e   men by mistake, it then goes on to explain how to distinguish one from the
other: 'Both officers and men wear well-cut uniforms similar in appearance. Non-
commissioned ranks wear the V-neck tunic and collar and tie that we associate
with an officer. How then are we to tell them apart?' Explanations follow. One of
the reasons the American enlisted man won hands down in the dating game was
simply because he had a 'walking out' uniform, whereas the British serviceman
h   to make do with the same rough, odorous woollen cloth for work and play. The
more relaxed military attitude of the American soldier is often mentioned, they
were far less worried about bending the rules than their British opposite numbers.
GIs thought nothing of giving lifts to civilians in Army vehicles, frequently
scooping up both girl and bicycle into a truck, besides allowing children, as we have
seen, into security areas.

Importantly, from the female point of view, the Americans did not recognise
class divisions in a society where one was judged by one's accent. This worked
both ways but it did result in many working class girls being taken to places
hitherto beyond their wildest dreams. Much has been said of the superiority of
the American courting techniques to that of the British, the likely end product of
the American co-educational system where boys were accustomed to being with
girls, and knew what they wanted to hear and how to please them. The majority
of these men were straight out of high school or in their first year at college,
young enough to go for sixteen- and seventeen-year-old British girls, for many
of whom it was their first experience of the opposite sex. Small wonder they
were dumbfounded by the good manners, generosity, exuberance and friendliness of these Yanks. To many of these impressionable young girls, knowing
nothing of the USA except through the cinema, it was Hollywood come to life.
Unfortunately, most were unaware of the American dating pattern by which
the boy went as far as he could: 'A really successful date is when a man asks
for everything and gets nothing' writes Margaret Mead, the American
anthropologist. The GIs, incidentally, were equally astounded at how often this
standard approach worked, though mostly it did not, for in the 1940s fear of
pregnancy or venereal disease was a major deterrent. Also, lack of opportunity
played a part, 'few of us had a place of our own, we either had watchful parents or
landladies'.

It was not just the young and unattached women who fell for their charms.
Lonely wives whose husbands had been away for years succumbed, and even
wives whose husbands were around. Then a child living in Clapham, one lady
remembers being dumped with neighbours every Wednesday afternoon while

her mother trotted to the West End to help entertain American officers at the Park Lane Hotel, precious nylon stockings a reward; her father seemed not to mind. A mature Bournemouth housewife, her husband at sea on Russian convoys, considered dancing with officers at the big hotel tea dances to be her 'war work'.

Many girls in their early teens were just not quite old enough, and often regretted this fact. Especially the young girls who lived in Huntingdon and heard that Clark Gable was in the area; one teenager swore she had travelled on the same bus. A thirteen-year-old who lived on a farm skirting an airfield was highly embarrassed when a GI told her she had 'kissable lips', she wasn't even sure what that meant. Equally disconcerted was a fifteen-year-old who when asked if she knew the 'Why dance', and answered in the negative, was promptly grabbed in a smoochy hold, and the GI said 'Why dance?' Being a total innocent unused to the company of men she was, to put it mildly, perturbed. As was the girl who was allowed to go to the pictures with a respectable GI her family had met through their church: 'He put his arm around me, I was petrified and sat rigidly upright for two hours.' Some schoolgirls of course were more sophisticated: a Cambridge girl recalls a sixth-former being expelled because an American fighter pilot buzzed the playing field. Olwen Evans, then taking her School Certificate, was fortunate enough to be a bridesmaid at her brother's wedding to an American girl, a variation on the more usual Anglo-American nuptials. The best man asked her out and her mother reluctantly gave permission. It was a one-off, but she boasted at school that she'd been out with a Yank, 'every girl's dream'. She also recounts the sad tale of a friend, 'short, plump and plain', who absented herself from school. When next seen, this girl was all tarted up and using heavy make-up: 'She had become a toy for the American soldiers, a camp follower, and was later expelled from school.'

Not everyone was smitten at first. Meg Thomas was then a young telephonist with the National Fire Service. She did not take to them straightaway and found them 'brash and full of themselves', but then came to appreciate the way they 'lit up the place with their generosity, quick wit and eagerness to help older people'. Significantly, she remained faithful to her fiancé in the Royal Navy, but did allow GIs to escort her occasionally. An intelligent girl, she was aware of the great diversities of culture and background of the GIs. She was very scathing of one dumb blonde who maintained that her Yank had a ranch waiting for him in New York 'and she believed him'. She, herself, once went out with a very shy, gentlemanly Jewish boy, and contrasts his attitude with that of another GI, who boasted that after the war he was going to be 'Somebody', his favourite saying being 'I ain't gonna be no Mediocre.'

Some say that the lower classes were the most hospitable and welcoming to the strangers (the reverse has also been said); the middle and upper certainly had their reservations. Harold Nicolson was not impressed by their gum chewing and lack of interest when he escorted a group around the House of Commons. Writer Naomi Mitchison, admittedly left wing and therefore anti-American by definition, says in December 1943, 'Nobody has a good word to say for them and the ones one sees about look mostly pretty awful.' She also quotes a Free French officer who said to her, 'I musn't think he behaved like an American. They do so hate the wretched Ameriques.' It was not entirely a class divide though. Richard Brown, an Ipswich draughtsman, writes in his diary somewhat waspishly in September 1943, 'the town now boasts about twenty or so Americans in twos or threes every time I go to work. They must be Yanks. I saw an officer sitting on the pavement in Princes Street today.' Strangely, although Ipswich is later awash with American servicemen, he rarely refers to them. Evelyn Waugh writes much the same thing: 'London was full of American soldiers, tall, slouching, friendly, woefully homesick young men who always seemed in search of somewhere to sit down.' Molly Panter-Downes, a London lady who kept a wartime diary, is much nicer. Her entry for 31 January 1942 reads, 'One of the few bright spots was the arrival of the American troops in Ulster, which cheered people enormously.'

Not everybody found the Americans smart and some people were actually put off by the appearance of some of the GIs: trousers that stretched tightly over 'big backsides', sloppiness and often uninhibited behaviour. The British were offended by the constant gum chewing and the fact that Americans still spat in the streets. They stared in wonderment at the American way of eating, fork in the right hand, as the knife underwent all kind of convolutions. Initially the British, of course, were as guilty of stereotyping their American allies as were the Americans of the British. All Americans were therefore 'forthcoming, impulsive and demonstrative'. Some people even thought them slightly effeminate because GIs wore aftershave, and seemed to be festooned with jewellery, gold watches, and wedding or class rings. In 1942, before the trickle of American servicemen became a flood, the British government set up an American Forces Liaison Division to coordinate the efforts of the regional and local authorities. The agency produced pamphlets that were similar to the American publications, all aimed at smoothing relations and promoting understanding between the two factions, but on most issues really doing very little and sitting uneasily on the fence. From the *Cambridge Daily News*: 'To these American boys Britain is a foreign land. Many of our customs and habits will be very strange . . . Just because we start with a feeling of kinship and because we share the same language, we are apt to be less understanding when we meet an American.'

Many British people found the American lack of reserve – the opposite of the stiff upper lip syndrome of the British – less than attractive. GIs would admit to homesickness, fear and loneliness. A British volunteer with the American Red Cross was astonished to see a man actually crying. Barry Goldsmith was equally astounded when a nineteen-year-old GI burst into tears because the family china cabinet reminded him of his grandmother's, 'back home'. Nor were they blooded in the ways of war: 'my father was most amused when the air raid siren went and the soldiers panicked'. So it has been said did the officers at Grosvenor House initially. Other newly arrived GIs obviously did not recognise the sound of the warning. Barry recalls the night when the sirens sounded in Southampton:

> We, like everyone else in the road, had gone down into the Anderson shelter, the Americans remained in their billets (school classrooms) with the doors and windows wide open and all the lights blazing. The man next door called across the fence to one of the American MPs and explained the black-out regulations. The MP, who was armed, called immediately for all the lights to be extinguished. He was answered by derisory whistles and rather rude comments. He did not ask a second time, but commenced to shoot out the light bulbs. After about the third shot it was panic stations, there was pandemonium as bodies in various stages of dress and undress rushed out into the darkness and fought to get into the shelters erected in the playground.

The waste of food at American bases appalled everybody, as did the half-smoked cigarettes and discarded drinks. The somewhat unpopular Gen John C.H. Lee (sometimes referred to as Jesus Christ Himself), head of Services of Supply, did clamp down on food waste, but it still happened. Someone remembered an entire ham being thrown out, more than a week's ration for a family. Eisenhower's aide, Harry Butcher, relates an incident when an American officer entered a hotel dining room (also patronised by the British) juggling two grapefruit. 'He ostentatiously had them cut, pulled a sack of sugar from his pocket and lavishly sprayed it over the grapefruit and the tablecloth. The CG [Eisenhower] condemned such a display as ungentlemanly . . . said if he had been present, he would immediately have ordered the officer home by slow boat, preferably unescorted.' When American ships tied up at British ports they deposited their designated waste in huge bins on the dockside. Bert Millgate remembers dock workers, and anyone else around, scavenging through these bins for anything worth the taking: half-eaten chicken carcasses and almost full tins of food. The very worst waste occurred when the camps were disbanded and the clearing-up crews were ordered to destroy everything. A boy living 17 miles from Swansea saw the red glow, which lasted for three days, of the mammoth bonfire. It was heartbreaking to see bulldozers crushing scarce bicycles, car parts, stainless steel cooking pots, and other unobtainable goods. GIs who had received hospitality from local families managed to 'spirit away' some of it. An Oxford family was astonished and delighted one day when a jeep arrived laden with tinned food, blankets, kitchen utensils and even an electric iron. The khaki blankets were in use for the next twenty years.

Many were the misunderstandings on both sides caused by differences in terminology. The incoming GI was forewarned of this: 'If invited to someone's flat, it's an apartment, don't refer to a tramp as a bum, or the pavement as the sidewalk, garbage is called rubbish, a girl is not a dame or – worse still – a broad, a wrench is a spanner, suspenders are braces and a vest is an item of underwear not a waistcoat. And American "pants" are trousers, often a cause of confusion.' The list is long; one GI was most offended when a well-meaning lady called him 'homely', which in American usage means ugly. The British were totally bemused by the constant use of the word 'ass' (as in posterior) – 'haul ass; kick ass'. But surely the most embarrassing for innocent young women was the use of the word 'rubber', not, they were to discover, something used to erase pencil marks. It was as difficult for a GI to understand regional accents as it was for the British to comprehend the widely disparate American inflections, ranging from Brooklynese to a Texan drawl. Not surprisingly, given the numbers of Americans swarming over the country, these linguistic differences mattered less and less as each absorbed something of the other.

Mothers of small children adored these men who made such a fuss of their children, schoolgirls not quite old enough to date mourned the fact, older women loved being called 'Ma'am', while older men often enjoyed their company. It was the young male who could be downright antagonistic to these 'friendly invaders'. Other Allied servicemen apart, it was the local lads who were unhappy with the considerable competition. They did not stand a chance once the GIs arrived, though truthfully there were probably few eligible men around by this time, except those medically unfit for service or in reserved occupations. Girls were used to partnering each other at the village hops. All that was to change.

Inevitably a proliferation of verses made the rounds. This cry from the heart, sent by Margaret Richardson, has often been quoted and rather sums it up.

Dear old England's not the same
We dreaded invasion – well it came,
But no, it's not the beastly Hun
The Goddam Yankee Army's come.
You'll see them in the train and bus
There isn't room for both of us.
We walk to let them have our seats
And then get run over by their Jeeps.

They moan about our lukewarm beer
Think beer's like water over here
But after drinking two or more
You'll find them lying on the floor.
And you should see them try to dance
They find a partner, start to prance
And when you're nearly dead
They stop and smile
'How'm I doin' Honey Chile?'
With admiration we would stare
At all the ribbons that they wear
And think of deeds both bold and daring
That earned the medals they are wearing.
Alas, they haven't fought the Hun
No glorious battles have they won
That ribbon just denotes
They've crossed the ocean,
brave men in boats.

They tell you they can shoot and fight
I must admit their shooting's fine
They shoot a darn good Yankee line
They love you dear, till death do part
You are their life, their love, their all,
And if you leave you'll break their heart.
And then they leave you, broken-hearted
You wait for mail that doesn't come
Then you realise, you're awful dumb.

CHAPTER 4

How They Lived

The contingency plans made before December 1941 were to be frequently amended. There was an immediate shortage of shipping space, trained men and a   output, but the skeleton was drawn and amazing advances were made in 1942. Gen Dwight D. 'Ike' Eisenhower – appointed Commanding General of the ETO – arrived in London with his friend and aide Capt Harry C. Butcher USNR who, fortunately for posterity, kept a diary. The Combined Chiefs of Staff, American and British, were already working closely together, unlike the totally separate command structures of the First World War. Ensconced in Grosvenor Square, where the switchboard was soon handling up to 6,000 calls daily, things moved rapidly and efficiently at American Command Headquarters. It had been agreed top priority was the build-up of the USAAF strategic bomber force in the British Isles, which would work in conjunction with RAF Bomber Command to destroy the German industrial base. The man who was to lead the newly formed 8th Air Force (Bomber Command) was Lt Gen Ira A. Eaker, who had flown into Hendon with his immediate staff as early as February. To accommodate the anticipated sixty Combat groups, seventy-five airfields would have to be conjured up from somewhere. Some, for example Duxford and Bassingbourn, were to be taken over from the RAF, but the majority would have to be constructed from scratch, and mostly in East Anglia. In fact by D-Day the 8th and 9th USAAF were to occupy – short or long term – 126 airfields.

Indigenous builders, such as John Laing & Son, with local and Irish labourers, had the experience; the land required was often scoured from rich farmland. Thorpe Abbotts in Norfolk, home to the 100th 'Bloody Hundreth' Bomb Group, and Hardwick, where the 93rd BG was based, are typical. Visit these sites now, with their admirable memorial museums, and visualise what was and what is now again, glorious open fields, back to farmland. Not so typical is Stansted in Essex, which became the largest USAAF base in England, and is now London's third airport. Bomber airfields were built to a standard plan, usually occupying 500 acres, with three runways in a triangular pattern, the longest of which was up to 6,000 ft. With that went 3½ miles of sewers plus the approximately 300

A fire truck at the ready. These men were from the 2028th Fire Fighting Platoon attached to the 355th Fighter Group. (Ken Wells)

buildings needed to house engineering shops, PX, radio shack, medical centre (including a doctor for each squadron), Quartermaster, Ordnance, offices, weather unit, Current Events room (at Eisenhower's request), chapel and clubhouses for all ranks. In addition, of course, was the living accommodation for the some 3,000 personnel thus generated. The impact of 3,000 healthy young men on the nearby villages, whether in Norfolk, Suffolk or Cambridgeshire, can well be imagined. Those airfields that accommodated fighter aircraft did not require such long concreted runways: Duxford for most of the war was still a grass airfield, although in 1944 the Americans were to lay Pierced Steel Planking (PSP) for the main runway.

So the early arrivals were the airfield constructors such as the US Army's 820th Engineer Battalion (Aviation), to which Robert Arbib belonged. Their job was to prepare Debach near Ipswich to receive the B–24 Liberator bombers of the 493rd BG. Arbib arrived in August 1942 to mud and latrine buckets. These GIs were the unlucky ones, they had perforce to live in tents until the Nissen huts were ready. 'A Nissen hut is not a difficult thing to build,' says Arbib, 'You put down a rectangle of concrete for a floor, you place spanning arched ribs across the longer dimension, bracing them with longitudinal stays. You cover inside and outside of these ribs with sheets of corrugated steel. You seal up the ends with bricks, wood or concrete. A couple of windows and a door at each end, and you are ready to take up residence.' The Nissen hut was standard living accommodation on the airfields (like most of the buildings, widely dispersed in case of enemy action) and the subject of a love-hate – mostly hate – relationship. They were always cold and damp, heated only by a stove in the middle; a small, inadequate stove for which there was never enough coal. The old hands got the bunks nearest the stove, while new arrivals were literally 'out in the cold'.

Just bearable in summer, in winter the conditions were freezing. Mud was constantly being churned up, winter or summer, by the ever-present jeeps, trucks and trailers. It was the damp the GIs came to associate with their sojourn in this country, the everlasting, all-pervading damp. For those living in tents, such as the airfield engineers and later many of the infantry assembling for D-Day,

Men of the 355th pose atop a B–26 Marauder and two P-51 Mustangs. (Ken Wells)

Above: A lesson in tactics from the boss. Lt Col William J. Cummings Jr demonstrates strategy to the pilots of the 355th at Steeple Morden. (Ken Wells)

Left: Briefing the 91st at Bassingbourn. (Vince Hemmings)

A familiar sight on every American airfield. When the 355th finally left Steeple Morden all the bicycles were taken to Bassingbourn and crushed by a steam roller. (Ken Wells)

the continual damp was a nightmare, especially on rainy nights. One ex-GI swears he suffered with a cold from the moment he arrived until the moment he left Britain. Men from the northern states such as Minnesota, accustomed to fiercely cold winters, could never understand why it felt so much colder here when the thermometer registered well above freezing. Used to central heating, they found the solitary Nissen hut stove laughable. On some bases toilet and shower blocks were installed before the main force arrived, so they sometimes got their hot showers. Others had to make do with icy concrete bath houses inadequately fuelled. In Sawston near Cambridge they were later to recall pitch-black mornings in the middle of winter 'struggling from bed to the bitterly cold ablutions block, they were numbed to the bone by icy blasts which, some men swore, blew directly and unimpeded from the frozen plains of central Russia'.

The lucky ones were those who took over pre-war ex-RAF or British Army quarters. The 91st BG moved into Bassingbourn (much to the chagrin of the WAAF personnel who were turfed out of their comfortable billets): a purpose-built base with central heating, permanent brick accommodation blocks and substantial married quarters, which were allocated to the USAAF NCOs and officers. Use was made of empty schools, warehouses, unfurnished houses, abandoned mills and factories and country mansions, the owners of which

It took sixteen ground personnel to support each man in the air. These ground crew members were based at Steeple Morden. (Ken Wells)

were not always compliant. Rudyard Kipling's daughter later refused to give up any of Wimpole Hall in Cambridgeshire for an American hospital, nor would she allow huts to be built in the grounds within her view. The hospital units were eventually erected where they could not be seen from the house. However, this was not the typical attitude of the majority and a great many country houses were used as hospitals, schools or military camps as necessary.

Official policy was against billeting in private houses, but as demand outran supply of accommodation it was inevitable. Often it was the officers in a liaison role or GIs on special courses who were initially billeted out. A young woman widowed with one son lived with her aunt in Cardiff, in whose house also resided two

Capt E. Frink of the 355th, August 1943. (Cambridgeshire Collection)

GIs, medical students completing their training at Cardiff University. They became uncles to her little boy and big brothers to the young widow, taking her to dances and parties: 'time you had a bit of fun'. One was rather a greedy young man, who consumed all the extra rations provided by the ever-generous US Army for Christmas, as the rest of the family ate their own meagre rations and watched. The GIs gave the grandfather a bottle of whisky, which he, a teetotaller, 'ceremoniously poured down the kitchen sink in front of them'. The mother of a nine-year-old girl in Swansea took in two soldiers when asked because they looked so young and she felt sorry for them. 'The American Army only expected the soldiers to sleep in our home, they were given meals at a local centre, but the people who had given them a room were paid a certain amount each week.' She was so disgusted with the small amount offered that she gave it back to the officers and kept the men for nothing. The American boys appreciated this and gave her any surplus food they could lay their hands on, the pure white bread making the greatest impression. However, householders' experiences were not all good. The captain billeted on a family in Cambridge took advantage of their absence to throw a party. When the family returned they found that all the beds had been used. Also when the hostess, in a kindly gesture, wrote to the wayward captain's wife back home she received a cutting reply to the effect that she assumed the lady was having an affair with her husband.

Probably the first contact the USAAF servicemen had with the native population was with the farmers whose very land they were despoiling. Some farmers were understandably bitter, but in most cases relations were quickly established. A 9th AF mechanic remembers their local farmer well, 'we traded cigarettes or candy bars for eggs each week. Funny fellow, always good for a chuckle and always wore a necktie while doing his chores. Not being too much of a country boy myself I was quite surprised to see him ankle deep in manure and thinking nothing of it, and smelling of it most of the time.' Fresh eggs were much in demand by the GIs, who loathed powdered eggs, and bartering thrived. Eggs and fresh milk were exchanged for the largesse from the PX: tinned fruit was the most popular, or items acquired legally or otherwise from the cookhouse. For the village children it was paradise and they quickly inveigled their way onto the bases – security did not seem to apply to children – and into the lives of their American friends. Nor was it long before the Yanks ambled down to the nearest pub.

When Arbib strolled into The Dog in Grundisburgh for the first time in 1942 he was warmly greeted. The presence of the Americans caused some excitement, particularly when they bought drinks all round (Arbib quotes one last round as being for forty-seven people). Once the novelty had worn off they were often resented for

Finding out about another fine English tradition, The Dove Inn at Burton Bradstock.
(IWM D20142)

drinking the pub dry, since beer like everything else was in short supply. English beer was much stronger than anything the GIs were used to and indeed, since most states still prohibited drinking under the age of twenty-one, the majority probably were not used to alcohol at all: 'The Americans didn't drink anything more than Coca-Cola – they were mostly straight out of school – so when they started drinking our beer it soon went to their heads, with dire results.' There were, of course, ugly incidents, more so in the towns, but the village pub did provide a happy meeting ground; so different from the soulless stateside bar. Relationships were established that flourish to this day, and preconceptions corrected on both sides. Hospitality was extended bilaterally, although some GIs never did find much to like about the British or their country, and some locals never took to the 'ruddy Yanks'. It takes a lot of individual experiences to make up a whole.

Then, of course, there were the girls. Once the airfields were established and manned the social side developed. Quonset huts, effectively large Nissen huts, were used for messing, clubs and the American Red Cross club. Often a hangar was put into service for dances and United Service Organization (USO) shows. Dances drew the girls like moths to a candleflame, the food served being for some the greatest attraction. 'Oh the FOOD, tinned peaches, cakes, cream cakes and in

Actor James Cagney visits the 355th at Steeple Morden. (Ken Wells)

the summer Barbecues.' One WAAF was eventually lured to a dance at a nearby US base when her friends brought back reports of the food served. So the next time she went, and spent the entire evening in the kitchen eating doughnuts (donuts) with the cooks. Everything is relative: Wanda Newby, then a young woman in north Italy as the Germans retreated, says much the same thing about the British troops who occupied Italy, 'The British soldiers seemed to be very popular with the inhabitants of Verona. They formed clubs and held tea dances to which the local girls were invited. . . . Tea dances with cakes, to us then the cakes were manna from heaven and the dances were the greatest of fun.'

The friendly outgoing GI could meet a girl in the queue for the fish and chip shop, one British tradition popular with the GIs, or in the queue for the cinema. He could chat up a girl on a bus, on a train, over the Post Office counter, handing out coffee and donuts on the base or because the girl's mother took in laundry. Arbib had a wonderful time driving around the Suffolk villages on official business, and developed a great admiration for the hard-working British girls, who also managed to play hard. He quotes a fellow GI who thought the village of Sudbury had more pretty girls per square foot than any town he'd ever seen. Some were not so enamoured, considering the local girls had bad teeth, looked shabby and smelt less than fresh. Deodorants were not in common use in wartime Britain and supplies of freshly laundered clothes not easily come by. Few homes had hot water on tap and the only washing 'machine' was a washtub, scrubbing board and liberal supply of elbow grease. Most GIs, however, were very happy to fraternise with the local talent which was 'Over Here'. Few girls ever received anything other than a superficial impression of GI life in Britain – the wonderful dances and cheery fresh-faced easy-going generous young men. Margaret Whiting, who went out with one of the gunners on the famous 'Memphis Belle', said there 'was never a word about their missions'. The girls only saw the bright side, unless a particular boyfriend was lost.

P-51s buzzing the tower at Steeple Morden. (Ken Wells)

Richard Brown in Ipswich was one of the many people living near airfields who counted the bombers overhead. On 18 August 1943 he writes, 'Yesterday evening we saw a homecoming of Fortresses, 136 of them. Many were going singly and only about 60 were in their squadron formation, suggesting they had been broken up. The target, we learned today, was Schweinfurt.' The people living on the perimeters of a particular air base were acutely aware of the losses, especially in the early days when many of the pilots were insufficiently trained and long-distance fighter cover was unavailable. There were horrendous accidents, apart from planes lost directly to enemy action. Planes collided after take-off because the pilot lost sight of his wing man in cloud, planes failed to lift off because of icy conditions or the loss of an engine, instruments were misread and sometimes the pilot just ran out of runway. A particularly dreadful accident occurred when new crews with the 490th BG at Eye near Peterborough collided when practising flying in formation, and wreckage was scattered for miles. A Liberator from the 486th BG at Sudbury crashed onto a farm, killing a boy as well as the entire crew. Two B-17s of the 94th Group returning to Rougham clipped each other when on final approach. One landed safely in a field of brussels sprouts, the other broke in two and crashed, killing the entire crew. The 94th carried out 325 missions and suffered 1,800 casualties, killed, missing, injured or captured. Of the total 153 aircraft missing, 27 were downed by accidents. On many stations the accident proportion was even higher.

The 91st provide a Guard of Honour at Bassingbourn. (Vince Hemmings)

Jessie Pym, whose family farmed very close to an airfield in Devon, and knew many of the men from the nearby base, heard a plane circling very low one night. 'The plane crashed over the hedge of our field, the pilot's body was in our field; he must have crashed very hard as the shape of his body with his arms outstretched stayed on the ground for many months; another body was found hanging from a tree with his parachute, two more bodies were found dead in another field.' The *Stars and Stripes* refers to a particularly tragic incident when the men who baled out of a crippled bomber died while the crew remaining on board belly landed the bomber and then walked away. The 100th BG at Thorpe Abbotts was dubbed the 'Bloody Hundredth' because of its high rate of losses, one of the worst incidents being the raid on Regensburg on 17 August 1943 when the group lost nine B-17s and, according to legend, foxed the Luftwaffe and thereafter became a special target. After the war this was proved to be untrue, but at the time it helped account for the particularly heavy casualty rate. On 8 October 1943 in a raid on Bremen the group lost 7 aircraft (72 men), but even worse was to come on 10 October when, of 13 aircraft, only a B-17, flown by Robert 'Rosie' Rosenthal, returned: 21 aircraft, with 200 men, gone in a single week. Some of those missing in action (MIA) did later turn up as prisoners of war and some even made it back to Britain with the help of the Dutch, French or

The 324th Bomb Squadron from Bassingbourn, September 1944. (Vince Hemmings)

A close shave. (Vince Hemmings)

Belgian resistance. A few were lucky, and landed in Sweden or Switzerland, but most did not. Maj Rosenthal flew a record fifty-two combat missions in eighteen months. He was shot down three times, twice landing in enemy territory and once in Russia, but managed to make it back to base each time.

Every Bomb Group suffered similiar losses. The fliers were the golden boys, as were RAF aircrew: they got flight pay, the best women and rapid, unseemly promotion into dead men's shoes. The night before a mission was a terrible strain and few could eat the pre-mission breakfast. They all remember feeling constantly cold and tired, 'the brassy taste of fear' and the sheer physical discomfort of flying for hours wearing an oxygen mask, 'chilled to the bone', throat aching and eyes burning. In spite of the protective clothing and heated suits there were many instances of frostbite. Almost even worse was the tension for a mission prepared and then scrubbed at the last moment because of bad weather. Harry Crosby, Group Navigator for the 100th, says that after every mission he was so exhausted he could hardly walk. They all had to suffer the loss of friends dead, severely wounded or MIA. There were instances where a crew did not last a single mission and therefore had no time even to make friends. Replacement crews came almost daily, with only one or two men remaining from the original squadron or group in a very short time. Sometimes the

The 91st BG were to suffer almost 2,000 casualties during their stay at Bassingbourn. (Vince Hemmings)

Another fails to get airborne, but luckily the pilot walked away, 26 November 1944. (Ken Wells)

A B-17 from nearby Bassingbourn crashed onto this P-51 of the 355th. (Ken Wells)

aircrew did not even have time to learn the name of their ground crew chief, or he theirs. Experiences in RAF Bomber Command mirror almost exactly those of the American fliers: the same fears, accidents, cancelled missions, closeness of the bomber crews, the unbelievable tension of facing that final mission, and the dedication of the ground crews.

Ground crews in the USAAF serviced specific aircraft. The 91st BG Crew Chief W. Hill's unit at Bassingbourn consisted of a total of nine men who were responsible for nine aircraft. When the planes returned from a mission they would assess the damage, tackle the easiest one first, then work all night until all aircraft were mission ready again. Major maintenance was done in huge hangars with special steel-plated doors, which were hopefully bomb proof. Ground crews, like the senior officers in the control tower, would anxiously await the homecoming planes – called 'sweating it out' – counting them in, and noting the red flares that indicated injured on board, but worst of all registering the gaps. Chief Hill said, in 1996, that he never got over seeing young men leave in the morning and not return. To the ground crew also went the grisly task of removing traces of dead fliers, something else they would never forget.

Not all ground crew were assigned particular aircraft. Mechanics were frequently sent to repair or collect and bring back, in a 40-ft trailer, planes that had come down away from the home base. Stan Kieffer, working with Mobile

Repairing the damage at Bassingbourn. (Vince Hemmings)

British girls and GIs work side by side repairing aero engines. (IWM D11801)

Repair and Reclamation, had to go to Dover to work on one of the 9th AF's A-20s. They pitched their tent near the edge of the cliffs and went off to look at the scenery – fortunately as it turned out. 'There was a lot of shouting behind us and, turning about, we saw this English Ack-Ack gun pit and everyone yelling at us to get down. They began shooting at something and brought down a V-1 directly overhead and we watched as the pieces rained down on our tent.'

Although these back-room boys were the unsung heroes – no special passes for them – the airfield ground crews and men of the numerous support services were usually the most permanent occupants of the bases. They were the ones who watched aircrew and commanders come and go, for few base commanders stayed longer than a year. So it was frequently the men of the maintenance and support groups who became closest to the local families and married the local girls, men like Eddie Graham of the 308th BG. As did GIs stationed at the permanent supply

Dispensing the coffee and donuts at Steeple Morden. (Ken Wells)

bases such as Burtonwood, the huge SOS base in Lancashire, Bovingdon Air Transport Supply Depot or assorted Headquarters staff, and those who worked in the hospitals. At Bristol, for instance, there were three American hospitals nearby, as well as a huge supply camp at neighbouring Bedminster. Americans flooded the town and port and many, of necessity, were billeted locally.

One group of men who were to stay two years was the 312 Signal Company, part of the 66th Fighter Wing headquarters based at Sawston Hall in Cambridgeshire. The stunning Elizabethan building itself contained the administrative nub of the Wing. Assorted buildings in the grounds and adjoining field, which included stables, the old manse and Boys Brigade hut, wooden huts (left over from RAF occupation) and a generous sprouting of the familiar Nissen huts became the domain of the 312th and housing for the enlisted men. Other men lived behind the Congregational church and the officers took over an empty house. Another, Brook House, became the Officers' Mess. Sawston was an industrial village, long associated with paper-making and tanning, and already filled to bursting point with evacuees and additional workers from the cities. It also, like many other East Anglian villages, lacked mains water and sewerage. The collection of night soil had only been recently instituted; some houses were still using privy pits. 'In the autumn of 1943 there were bad smells in Sawston High Street. Gullies were blocked, sewers overloaded. 350 soldiers coming to live in the village could really gum up the works.' Not what the newcomers were accustomed to at all. Also, the Hall and grounds were smack in the village centre, which was thus overrun by American personnel and their transport: staff cars, jeeps, trucks and bicycles. The men had literally only to cross the street to the nearest pub – there were four pubs within 100 yds – or to the 'Clubmobile', an old Greyhound bus, parked in a pub yard. These Clubmobiles were a godsend to all GIs on bases not large enough for the full treatment Red Cross club. They were usually staffed by three girls, in this case two British and one American, who got up at the crack of dawn to dispense home-made donuts and coffee. Other Clubmobiles had bunks fitted so that they were completely self-contained units. Sometimes a NAAFI van provided the service, probably without donuts, but welcome nonetheless.

The infantry divisions who poured into the British Isles for D-Day often had it a lot rougher. If they took over British Army barracks such as Tidworth it was not so bad, at least the basics were in place. A unit might get lucky and occupy a school building or even be assigned a private billet, but mostly it was tents and latrine buckets. A few days before 6 June 1944 most moved to staging areas and were confined behind barbed wire to ensure security. 'We all knew the invasion was near,' says Jules Honig, combat engineer with the 294th, 'the food quality improved 100%.' Instead of powdered eggs and corned beef hash they were fattened up for the kill with fresh eggs for breakfast and steak and french fries for dinner. The miracle is that the organisation stood up to this greatest test and managed to house and feed the literally millions of GIs involved in the great venture. These men did not have much time to play.

CHAPTER 5

How They Played

So what did the GI do when he was off duty? There were different levels of recreation time. After duty men might visit a pub, sample local hospitality or take the liberty truck into the nearest town, leaving at 7 p.m. and returning at 11 p.m. Then there was the 'Pass', usually two or three days, particularly for aircrew deemed to need more rest and recreation than most. Finally there was the 'furlough', anything up to eight days, when the majority hit the big city, London, wherever possible. When a base was equipped with clubrooms and able to organise its own dances, parties and shows, there were those who chose not to venture outside this Little America.

The aforementioned pub was frequently the first point of contact, because it was the most accessible and represented the quickest way to relax. English beer, warm, weak and watery, was the one thing all GIs remember, many with disgust, but equally many worked at getting used to it. George Rosie spent a lot of time in the pubs, loved the atmosphere and reckoned he played about 900 games of darts with elderly locals for a pint, and never once won. The arrival of the GIs did pose something of a dilemma for the pub regulars. In the villages the first few Americans were often regarded with suspicion, but then welcomed for their warmth and generosity, even if they did sometimes consume all the available supplies. Many GIs gradually became accustomed to the beer because there was not much else on offer: spirits, preferably whisky, being even harder to get hold of. Others still recall English beer with a shudder. Capt Butcher relates Al Jolson's remark at a *Stars and Stripes* cocktail party, 'The beer is lousy, why don't they put it back in the horse?'

In the nearby towns there were favoured service drinking spots, some like The Eagle in Cambridge, where USAAF and RAF mixed amicably, both groups writing their names with candle soot on the now-famous ceiling, still to be seen thanks to the efforts of enthusiasts such as James Chainey. It was not all beer and skittles, however, and alcohol-induced aggression frequently flared up into fisticuffs in the hostelries of the larger towns and ports, but in the village pub the landlord was firmly in control. Not all GIs were drinkers and some were not always happy with their fellows. 'Found many of the US servicemen very rude and some quite nasty, especially the drunks.' The Americans virtually took over The Bull in Totnes where the landlord allowed GIs to serve behind the bar. It was very much a mutual support group since the landlord collected swill for his pigs from the various American barracks, and also ran a taxi service that was much to the benefit of the local GIs. Some Americans developed a real taste for English beer; a Mosquito pilot who stayed in the USAAF after the war could not wait to get a posting back to Britain for his 'pint'. This item which appeared in the Hash Marks column of *Stars and Stripes* sums it up:

> Drinking Bitters gives me jitters
> Supping ale turns me pale
> Guzzling mild I act like a child
> Soaking up gin I feel all in
> My nightly missions I've had to scrub
> Goodbye, goodbye O hallowed Pub.

The village pub, however, would not usually be the place to meet girls, although wartime circumstances did change things a bit. But as Howard Campbell puts it, 'most of my buddies went for the beer and broads'. And mostly the 'broads' were to be found at dances. Everybody danced and in the towns there would probably be one going on somewhere almost nightly, even several on one night. Tea dances – the very term lends an air of respectability – were particularly popular, especially at the Officers' Clubs. In Bournemouth the Marsham Court Tea Dances were a favourite rendezvous for interested parties. There were dances on base for which invitations were issued en bloc to any nearby source of females. There were dances at the American Red Cross clubs (selected young ladies only), dances organised by the town council, English-Speaking Union (ESU), Women's Voluntary Service et al., and the village hop where teenagers and older people would join in.

Hilda Graham lived near Grafton Underwood (97th BG), and helped serve coffee and sandwiches at the dances held at the Aero Club. Like every female for miles around she had heard that Clark Gable was in the area (he was at Polebrook):

Every week we held a couple of dances at the Raven Hall in Corby and the rumours always got started that Clark would attend. He never did show up, but one night a GI friend of ours who had the use of his officer's car came to the dance and parked outside. Now it so happened that this friend of ours looked

One famous air gunner. Clark Gable manning a gun on a B-17. (Vince Hemmings)

quite a lot like Clark Gable, moustache and all, so we spread the rumour that Clark was outside and would sign autographs. It wasn't long before a line formed up in the parking lot and our friend was signing slips of paper and anything that could be written on. It was very dark outside and I must admit that in the dim light our friend did look the real McCoy. There was hardly anyone left dancing as everybody scrambled to get this 'famous autograph'.

In Britain to promote the role of gunner, Clark Gable did actually train as such and flew several missions. He was apparently a pleasant, quiet man who traversed the area on a motor bike, trying very hard to maintain as low a profile as possible in view of his publicity role.

Officially, at dances on the base no alcohol was served, the great attraction being the food, the music and the dancing itself. Dancing so totally unlike the orderly English way, with all the couples moving in one direction so as not to bump into anybody else. 'The whole dance floor is a rotating mass of people all dancing in the same direction, it would be insane to try and dance against the stream.' recalls Harold Hennessey, 'Americans danced freelance.' They seemed to either dance cheek to cheek or jitterbug. Such dancing, also known as jiving, had been infiltrating the dance floor here and there before 1942, but when

Capt Clark Gable at Polebrook with two lucky girls, Delma Northern and Mavis Pollard.
(Michael Downes)

The Glen Miller band plays in a hangar at Steeple Morden, August 1944. Glen is third from the left. (Ken Wells)

The 355th FG's own 'Fighter Comets'. (Ken Wells)

the GIs moved in there was no holding back. To young British girls it was the movies come to life: Mickey Rooney, Judy Garland and the American high-school scene. And it was such fun. All problems vanished when you were hurtling round the dance floor or flying over your partner's head. It took a lot of energy and was good for anything that ailed, 'dancing always got rid of my chilblains'. Since the majority of the Americans were under twenty-one this excess of energy was understandable.

The music was equally fantastic. Many service units were able to gather together a selection of professional musicians and gifted amateurs. The RAF had the 'Squadronnaires' and most large USAAF bases fielded their own dance band. Some, like the 355th FG 'Fighter Comets', were famous and much in demand elsewhere. Duxford had the 'Thunderbolts', Debden 'The Flying Eagles' and there were countless others. A thirteen-year-old girl from Bottisham used to watch enviously through the windows at the antics of the 361st FG, 'My, those Americans could dance.' To add to the excitement were the visiting dance bands and singers from the USA. If girls were not attracted by the men and the music at the dances on base the lure of the food was overwhelming. 'Huge cream cakes, chocolates,' Vi Crook remembers, 'the tinned peaches and fruit cake and

Coca-Cola, small gifts of flowers and cigarettes. You were perfectly safe unless you went outside for a breath of fresh air.' Opinions are forever divided. There are those who say the majority of the GIs behaved in a gentlemanly fashion and would take 'No' for an answer. Others say the opposite and maintain that the GIs were only after 'one thing'. Both, of course, were true. Walking home one day a seventeen-year-old in Coventry got chatted up by a seemingly very pleasant young GI until, that is, he tried to push her into an air-raid shelter. It frightened her off Americans for good. Another girl was set upon by the Medical Officer who was ostensibly escorting her home in his jeep after she became ill at a base dance: 'more hands than an octopus'. There were, however, a surprising number of platonic relationships, men just happy to be in female company while remaining faithful to the girl at home. It is absurd to attempt to stereotype, although it is often said that the married men were the worst. Certainly a very large proportion of the younger men were as virginal as the girls they were trying to seduce. A very long way from home, perhaps afraid and miserable, but trying to tough it out. Drink helped and so did female company.

At public dances the situation was often less easy. Different nationalities, in and out of uniform and in combination with the availability of alcohol, could trigger nasty incidents if the event was not properly supervised. The situation often worked itself out, the Americans patronising one dance hall, the British servicemen another. One girl remembers the liberty trucks outside the Guildhall in Cambridge – famous for its dances, and usually patronised by locals and British servicemen – trying to poach girls for dances on the base. Unlike the British services, officers and men of an airplane crew would socialise off duty and descend upon the nearest town in a group, 'as a family' going to the pub, dancing or a cinema.

In the war years everybody went to the cinema and it was one form of official entertainment that was not in short supply. The programme ran continuously, always consisting of two features plus the news and, if you were lucky, an organist in the interval. Most cinemas changed the programmes mid-week, so in a decent sized town it would be possible to go every day without repetition. Old ladies took sandwiches and sat in the front, courting couples made for the back row. The GIs could afford the best seats in the balcony, while some cinemas even had special two-seater boxes for the courting couples. It was a haven of cosiness in the dark, even if the film was viewed through the blue fog of tobacco smoke. 'Theatres with ashtrays in the armrests' astonished the boys from the USA, where smoking was forbidden in all theatres. In the more relaxed wartime atmosphere many a romance started in the cinema queue. When the liberty trucks poured into town in the evening some of the men who were not drinkers or did not fancy their chances at the dance hall would head for a picture house, 'Rather felt I hadn't a chance, so soon started going to the cinema.'

As the American Red Cross established its clubs both on and off the bases many GIs stayed within these confines. The ARC clubs were usually run by American civilians, paid or otherwise, with the help of local volunteers. These local girls had to be recommended by a reputable person and then vetted. They were given identity cards and closely supervised. Any girl leaving the premises with a patron would have her pass withdrawn. This did not, of course, prevent them from arranging dates and many a 'volunteer' became a GI bride. Of the estimated 27,000 ARC club workers in Britain in 1944, 25,000 were British and half of them volunteers (a quarter of the cost incurred was paid by the British as reverse Lend-Lease). Mrs Harvey worked a 4-hour shift two days a week at the ARC club in Belfast: 'It is reckoned that 200,000 US servicemen were stationed in the province. The headquarters of the ARC was originally called the Plaza, a ballroom and skating rink. The ballroom had excellent visiting American bands and what were called "Hostesses" to jitterbug with. Shortly before his death Glenn Miller's band gave a wonderful performance. He visited the canteen and I was fortunate enough to procure his autograph. Shortly after he went missing over the English Channel.'

The Cambridge ARC club on King's Parade. (Cambridgeshire Collection)

Celebrity line-up at the Polebrook American Red Cross club. (Michael Downes)

The best-known American Red Cross club was, of course, Rainbow Corner on the corner of Shaftesbury Avenue, where a Lyons Corner House and Del Monico's restaurant used to be. It was a mecca for every American serviceman this side of the ocean. With a staff of 450 it had opened in November 1942 in a blaze of publicity. It was equipped to serve as many as 7,000 meals daily. Bed and breakfast cost 2s 6d, lunch or supper 1s and two cakes could be had for 6d. The club was open 24 hours a day, boasted a gym, juke box, barber shop and the 'finest handball court in the British Isles'. As well as acting as an information centre it provided a library, writing room, games room, classes in everything from art to archery, concerts and movies. Innumerable reunions, children's parties, dinners and sporting events were held at Rainbow Corner, as were the star-studded USO shows. The Columbia Club in Seymour Street had 700 beds. Depending on the size all the ARC clubs provided some of the aforementioned, even if it was only coffee and donuts and newspapers from home.

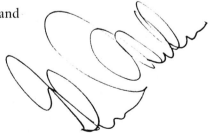

Glen Miller's autograph. (Mrs B. Harvey)

Royston Museum, formerly the Congregational Sunday school and American Red Cross club. (Author)

Kathleen Dodkin was, from its opening in 1942, secretary to the American Red Cross director of the Royston ARC Club, in premises taken over from the local Congregational church (now Royston Museum). Before the club opened for business a shower block and washroom was installed and the kitchen modernised beyond belief, complete with waffle irons and stainless-steel equipment. The set-up was very professional; permanent staff included an assistant director, handyman, accountant, cook and a housekeeper. Open seven days a week, 12 hours daily, the atmosphere at the club was always lively and intense, says Mrs Dodkin. The patrons were young and many were aircrew, always conscious of the fact that each visit might be the last. The staff had to harden themselves to unexplained absences and learned to comfort the survivors. 'Quite often boys would come to my office to cry on my shoulder.' There were also naturally many amusing incidents. 'The club porter kept a supply of condoms to hand out as necessary. One day when the porter was absent a GI requested a 'rubber' from the innocent girl manning the Reception Desk. She went and got him a plaster and asked if he would like her to put it on for him!' The Royston ARC Club was large and well equipped, with room enough for films, dances and billiards besides the customary reading and quiet rooms. Open to enlisted men only, officers and other Allied servicemen were only permitted when guests of an enlisted man. Some clubs were particularly venturesome: that in Northampton arranged trips to Stratford, and had its own string ensemble as well as providing the usual foreign language, bridge and dancing classes. Officers had their own clubs, the most prestigious being Grosvenor House in London, where a meal cost 2s 6d and the hostesses

The Donut Club, Ashford, Kent. (*Kent Messenger*)

Keeping up with the news from home. Servicemen relax at the Donut Club in Ashford, Kent.
(*Kent Messenger*)

there quite likely to bump into the Supreme Commander himself. Hotels like the Dorchester and Savoy were also the haunts of senior US Army officers, and those attracted to them.

In addition ARC clubs acted as clearing houses for offers of local hospitality, and arranged a vast number of visits. Organisations such as the Salvation Army, the Young Men's Christian Association (YMCA), Rotary Clubs and Jewish Hospitality Committees established social clubs. The churches and associated clubs provided a good meeting ground, and added a sense of decorum to relationships formed. It was deemed preferable to being 'picked-up' at a dance, and like was more likely to meet like. Parents would certainly have fewer objections if a daughter met a GI at church. The British were surprised by the number of American servicemen who did attend church services, especially the Catholics. The WVS alone ran some 200 Welcome Clubs where local citizens could meet up with GIs in a relaxed and friendly way and get acquainted with 'suitable' girls. In Cambridge the English–Speaking Union set up an information centre for American service visitors in October 1942, and was immediately overwhelmed by offers of hospitality.

The hospitality pack. This might have contained tinned fruit, sugar, fruit juices, coffee, rice and evaporated milk. (IWM EA10182)

Any soldier accepting one of these offers over the Christmas period of 1942 was to be given a ration pack for each day consisting of evaporated milk, sugar, coffee, rice, fruit juice etc., as available. Joan Andrews remembers an appeal for hospitality being made in church on Christmas morning 1944. Two GIs came to tea, one had two children of his own and could not take his eyes off Joan's small children. She wrote to the wives, parcels arrived and another lifelong friendship was formed. A boy whose young sister had scarlet fever and needed fresh fruit cycled hopefully down to a nearby park, where black troops were camped. The guard, 'a giant of a man', started talking to him and when hearing of the sister's illness told him to come back next day. He did so, and the soldier gave him a bag of oranges, rare luxuries, and some juice. The boy's mother then invited the soldier and friends to tea and another good relationship blossomed, although in this case there were 'a few raised eyebrows from the neighbours. But we could not have met nicer people.' Barry Goldsmith, whose house backed onto barracks for Southampton Docks, writes, 'Many of the Americans were homesick and would call over the fence, wanting just to talk; it wasn't long before they persuaded the local women to do their laundry. This they would pass over the fence along with all sorts of goodies such as cigarettes, gum and candy. The next thing I can remember is that my parents were inviting some of them round in the evenings. We would have five or six all crowded round us talking about their homes and families.' Barry's family had some great evenings, with sing-songs round the piano, and his father taught the GIs to play darts. One of them was a carpenter and made his mother an ironing board. Another liked to help his father in the garden and, their most regular visitor, bought Barry his first dog. This was the best kind of hospitality, spontaneous and from the heart.

Hospitality obviously took many forms. Two sisters, members of the WVS, husbands in the Army, did shifts manning the NAAFI canteen at a railway station. One of their assorted children remembers 'lots' of GIs being brought back to the house and wild parties round the piano until very late. The children would be sent to bed and bribed with chocolate to stay there. It was probably all innocent fun, but years later a lot of elderly ladies may have had a quiet

WACs sightseeing in Cambridge. (Vince Hemmings)

chuckle. Much of the officially organised effort went astray. A lot of GIs could not be bothered with the hospitality, probably felt it would be too much of an effort to comply with the plethora of instructions issued about such visits, nor were they interested in widening their horizons. Many 'chickened out' at the last moment. One Christmas there were 50 per cent 'no shows', which was very galling for the would-be hosts. Officers got the best official invitations, although the grand houses – with a few notable exceptions – were somewhat select-ive. One lovely story, with many variations, went the rounds: of the invitation issued by one exalted lady who intimated that she would condescend to entertain six GIs to tea, and stipulated 'no Jews'. At the appointed hour six very large and very black GIs arrived, saying that Col Cohen had sent them.

Capt David Kieffer punts along the Cam after being wounded in France. (Stan Kieffer)

There was an enthusiasm for sightseeing, especially in London where apparently Madame Tussauds was top of the list and Buckingham Palace and the Houses of Parliament ran close seconds. John Costello was taken on a tour of the sights by 'two young ladies with the British forces who loved their city, and were proud to show strangers its beauty, tradition and charm'. He was particularly thrilled by Westminster Abbey, with its memorials to famous men of literature, and watching WRNS 'do perfect close order drill' outside the Houses of Parliament. In Cambridge GIs asked for a guide

Taking the guided tour of Oxford, the Allies pass each other by. (IWM D19141)

to the colleges, having seen the film *A Yank at Oxford*. For many it was the quick tourist once-over, something they took in briefly in intervals during the serious pursuit of pleasure. Not all: a young officer assigned to Air Transport Command, spending time in London while awaiting a posting, visited as many places of interest as he could, trying to get to know the city. For the serious tourist it was a dream come true, with trips to Oxford and Cambridge a must, one nominated the Cambridge Backs as the most beautiful half-mile in England. During the university vacation both these renowned institutions offered one-week courses to interested GIs, £3 12*s* for officers, £1 12*s* for enlisted men. University dons offered erudite conversation and lectures were organised by all and sundry, with many university lectures open to the public, and some GIs did attend. A Cambridge

Three men from the Twin Cities: Stan Kieffer, Buddy Rosen and Dave Johnson meet up in Cambridge. (Stan Kieffer)

schoolgirl remembers US officers, educators no doubt, being shown around her showcase school on more than one occasion.

Large numbers of American servicemen had little or no opportunity to explore during a brief stay in the British Isles, others had the opportunity but little time or inclination. In the opinion of Edwin Sippel, an ATC pilot, who loved everything about Britain, it was basically a question of age; the mostly very young GIs were not interested in expanding their horizons. Some did take the trouble to walk the London streets, appreciate the many parks or take a trip on the Underground and go further afield. George Rosie took an unforgettable train ride to Scotland to visit relatives, which he termed the journey of a lifetime. Others had to traverse the country on official business, and loved what they saw, especially away from the big, shabby cities. But for the majority life was divided squarely between work, rest and play.

Play, apart from 'beer and broads', did include sport. Most airfields and camps boasted a baseball diamond of sorts, football pitch and softball court. At Rainbow Corner there were inter-service boxing tournaments, and Green Park off Piccadilly was literally taken over by baseball-playing Americans. An Army versus Navy

All friends together at a cricket match at Steeple Morden. (Ken Wells)

(American) football game was played at the White City in November 1944. At Cambridge there was a tripartite athletics meeting between the University, RAF and USAAF which was won by the RAF. The commander at Sawston Hall, sending news to some of his men in Germany in the spring of 1945, writes 'about thirty men have tried out for the softball team and many of the men are training for the track meet'. For recreation there was also music, apart from the dance bands. The Negro Choir particularly was in great demand, going on tour with the RAF Symphony Orchestra and performing at Liverpool Cathedral. In July 1943 Tech/Sgt Hugo Weisgall conducted the BBC Symphony Orchestra in a first performance of his own work at The Proms, and later a 2nd Lt was guest pianist with the London Symphony. The GI Music and Dance Revue toured British war factories and performed at children's parties. At the top end of the scale were the USO shows which visited the bigger bases and ARC clubs with shows that often featured big Hollywood names, such as Bob Hope, Frances Langford, Fred Astaire, Bing Crosby and James Cagney.

The Americans loved to throw a party. Besides the wonderful children's parties, they threw parties for Thanksgiving, Valentine's Day, Christmas, of course, and frequently to celebrate the completion of a number of missions. The 91st BG marked its second anniversary at Bassingbourn on Sunday 17 September 1944

The 91st BG's second anniversary party, complete with fun fair and 2,000 visitors. (Vince Hemmings)

The anniversary celebrations lasted three days. (Vince Hemmings)

with a grand party for 2,000 visitors, which went on from 10 a.m. until midnight. A 91st veteran remembers, 'Some 3,000 gallons of beer helped give the party a cheery atmosphere, and the hard liquor served at the Officers' Club, while limited in amount, was sufficient to give everyone a good time. Outside a broken arm or two there were no casualties, although one woman came very near to giving birth.' A fun fair was installed on the rugby pitch and two bands took turns to play in a hangar. Some party, and lucky locals. The 100th BG at Thorpe Abbotts celebrated first its 100th and then its 200th mission in much the same way. After these parties it was not unusual for girls to be winkled-out days later; it was not easy to keep track of hundreds of visitors and 3,000 men.

Girls had to be the most popular form of entertainment, and came in all shapes and sizes, anything between fifteen and fifty was said to be fair game. There is no doubt that the dances on American bases were a magnet to many girls. Young girls who in wartime lacked sufficient supervision, girls on war work away from home for the first time, nice girls and not-so-nice girls could not help but be attracted to the glamorous men, dancing to first-rate bands and food into the bargain. The girls who climbed aboard the liberty trucks on a Saturday night

Dancing with the big girls; entertaining WAAFS and ATS. (IWM HU55851)

did attract a lot of muttered disapproval. GIs apparently preferred blondes and the sale of peroxide soared. In the rural areas girls from the villages had had little in the way of entertainment before the Yanks arrived, so the dances and entertainments organised at the airfields were sheer heaven. The hostels where Land Girls lived were besieged; mass invitations went out to the WAAF and ATS barracks, nurses' homes and similar establishments for young ladies. It was not just the men who felt that there might not be a tomorrow, or were lonely, homesick and scared. Each used the other, but that is not to deny that many long-term relationships were established. After all, an estimated 70,000 British girls married GIs during and just after the war, and overall there were probably more nice guys than predators. As Harry Crosby says, 'these were good years for us to enjoy women'.

Some Americans did find entertainment and solace with their own women, perhaps the American Red Cross ladies, though many of those were already married or labelled as hunting for husbands. There were, of course, the WACs, but at their peak there were only about 4,000 in Britain. The influx of American nurses into this country in preparation for D-Day did not make a lot of difference to the average GI as they were for officers only. The few all-American weddings that did take place were usually between couples who had known each other 'back home'.

The GIs were not always out and about and a lot of time was spent in camp solely in the company of other men. They wrote letters, read, 'chewed the fat' and sometimes got on each other's nerves. They also gambled, and those who did were fond of 'shooting craps' (an expression that rather puzzled the British), playing cards – poker, pontoon, bridge – and most bases would have some facility to 'shoot pool'. All traps for the unwary beginner and a possible source of friction. For regardless of the fact that they were all Americans, proud to be so and fighting the same enemy, they were composed of disparate groups from different backgrounds, different religions and differing heritages with their own inbuilt prejudices. In some cases the American Civil War was still being fought, there was anti-Semitism and also city boy versus country hick. Most of the time these feelings would be kept in check: they did, after all, have a war to win.

CHAPTER 6

Problems

Apart from the fact that the GIs had the reputation of taking all the women and drinking all the available booze, the most serious grounds for falling out between the host nation and the American servicemen was the treatment of black soldiers by their fellow GIs. The blacks wondered at times who it was they were supposed to be fighting. In 1942 the British government teetered indecisively, desperate not to offend their Allies and equally anxious not to antagonise their own citizens. Some fairly pathetic excuses were given, such as it would be too cold for blacks in Britain and that, in the words of Sir James Grigg, the Secretary of State for War, 'they lacked the white man's ability to think and act to a plan'. Grigg was all for doing it the American way – total segregation – but Lord Cranborne, Secretary of State for the Colonies, to his credit refused to go along with that policy, pointing out that there were 10,000 West Indians in the RAF, all volunteers. The British government, the Church and military would have preferred to evade the entire issue by not having any black troops in Britain at all. However, most of the engineer battalions consisted of black soldiers, they worked at the docks, built airfields and manned the laundries and kitchens. The ETO could hardly function without them.

The official American line was to aim for a one-in-ten ratio black to white. A directive sent to the American Red Cross in London stated that black soldiers would be given the same leave and passes as the white troops, but that they should occupy separate dormitories and eat at separate tables where possible. Gen Eisenhower did his best: he stipulated that black GIs were to have equality of treatment 'but there would be segregation where facilities afforded. The coloured troops were to have everything as good as the white.' He also removed the existing censorship on articles covering stories about black troops.

A small boy in Belfast probably saw the first black GIs to arrive in Britain in 1942: 'The first wave of troops were white soldiers, the second were blacks. This was the first time I was confronted by segregation. For the first time in their lives negroes were riding in buses with white people, not all white soldiers were happy with this arrangement, and this was my first experience of racial prejudice.' A youngster from South Wales recalls, 'a fair amount of negroes. For some reason my mother warned my sister and I about these negro soldiers. Because I misunderstood her she laughingly told people that her son was under the impression that these negroes were fighting against us!' Another girl, then living near Dorchester, recollects 'one time there were several units of coloured soldiers in the camps. We, of course, had never seen coloured people before, and the day they arrived my friend, who lived down a dark lane, would not go home on her own, so my mother, who was always up for a good laugh, donned father's big boots and we walked my friend down the lane with my mother stomping along as hard as she could to make out there was a man with us! I must say these coloured soldiers were most polite and friendly, we felt a bit silly, re the big boots.' Probably during the D-Day build-up, one incident in Hampshire was always remembered by a lady now in her eighty-sixth year: 'I was pushing my two youngest children aged two and four along the main road which was absolutely packed with American servicemen both white and black. A tall, broad, black serviceman crossed the road and asked me if I would object to him pushing the pram for a while, it would be a reminder of his own kids. He pushed my children for about a mile, almost to my house, then thanked me very much, emptied his pockets of chocolate bars into the pram, and turned back up the road to join the convoy. That soldier's kindness was a rare treat for our children, as money was very scarce, but I'll never forget him and would like to think he survived the war.'

The problem was that the British did not know what to expect. Unless they lived near a port, large city or university town they had probably never encountered coloured people before. They were horrified when they saw how the blacks were treated by their own people, and although publicans, restaurant owners and the like had to pander to the majority of white American servicemen, most people sympathised with the blacks. Some even weighed in on their behalf; as did British Commandos in the infamous Battle of Mount Street in Wrexham. There were other pitched battles between white and black but not many that made the headlines; obviously such incidents would be suppressed by the censors where possible. Onlookers always remembered the brutality with which American MPs broke up these brawls, brutality usually aimed at the blacks. The British Army's Commanding Officer at Cardiff Barracks never forgot the occasion when nearby black troops, protesting over pay and conditions, barricaded themselves into their quarters. Their white officers went in with bull whips to sort them out.

In a way it was understandable that whites from the southern states would refuse to sit in the same restaurant, ride the same bus or share a pub or dance hall with the blacks, because that was all they knew. But northerners too had their prejudices, and one thing that no white American could bear was to see a white woman in the company of a black man. One girl always remembered the furore when she happened to mention to her sister's American fiancé, from one of the northern states, that the sister had danced with a black man, albeit not an American. There were some very unpleasant incidents: Leary Constantine, the famous West Indian cricketer, was asked to leave a hotel restaurant because GIs objected to his presence. Other West Indian servicemen were often victimised, as were the West Indian civilians over here on specific war work. A system was evolved where passes would be issued to white and black GIs so that they would be in town on alternate nights. To avoid trouble both groups tended to patronise different pubs and dance halls. There was a telling scene in the film *Yanks* where white GIs ganged up on a group of blacks, and this was not entirely fiction. It is also true that the 'black' pubs and dance halls were usually in the less salubrious parts of a town. A Royal Navy man, home on leave, recalls a white GI saying to the landlord of his local, 'I hope you don't serve any black American soldiers.' John Costello, an American infantryman en route to North Africa in 1942, writes about a transit camp near Liverpool: 'Our staging area was surrounded by barbed wire, it was just as well because our cultures clashed on our second day in England, and the British people had no idea what the fuss was about. Our negro people were not seen in public with a white woman. Of course it happened in a pub, when a girl with negro soldiers asked a white GI what he was staring at. Bad question, bad GI to answer the question – being from the Deep South. It spilled out onto the street, reinforcements were obtained for both sides, an outnumbered Bobby could not quell the anger, but a Recon Lieutenant, plus Tommy Gun and Recon support troops stopped the mêlée.'

The American Red Cross had segregated clubs, and the WVS toed the party line, establishing the Silver Birch Clubs for black GIs, the Welcome Clubs being for whites only. Dennis Green's family became involved with black Americans after a performance by members of the US Army Negro Chorus at their local church. His mother became a chaperone at the club for black GIs in Ipswich and Dennis, then an RAF officer, was always welcomed, as being a British white officer he 'wasn't bound by their segregation rules'. The club was also used by West Indians in the RAF.

It is frequently stated that many British preferred the black GIs to their white countrymen; they were generally acknowledged to be well mannered, pleasant and low key, less pushy and boisterous and were marvellous dancers. Their choirs were certainly much in demand, the *Stars and Stripes* reports a Negro choir touring

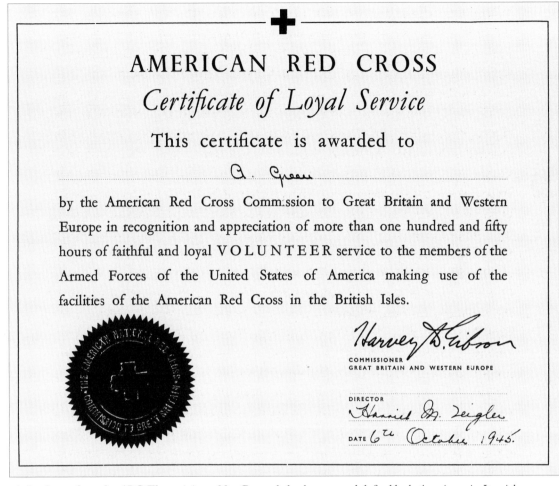

AMERICAN RED CROSS
Certificate of Loyal Service
This certificate is awarded to

G. Green

by the American Red Cross Commission to Great Britain and Western Europe in recognition and appreciation of more than one hundred and fifty hours of faithful and loyal V O L U N T E E R service to the members of the Armed Forces of the United States of America making use of the facilities of the American Red Cross in the British Isles.

Harvey D. Gibson
COMMISSIONER
GREAT BRITAIN AND WESTERN EUROPE

DIRECTOR
Harriet M. Zeigler
DATE 6th October 1945.

A thank you from the ARC. The recipient, Mrs Green, helped out at a club for black Americans in Ipswich.
(D. Green)

with the RAF Symphony Orchestra. The choir also performed with the London Symphony Orchestra and they sang in many cathedrals. The blacks probably trod cautiously, unable to believe their luck. In Britain they did not have to step off the pavement if a white person was approaching, nor were they obliged to relinquish a seat and stand on a bus. Graham Smith quotes the pub notice that stated 'For British people and Coloured Americans only', and the farmer who said 'I love the Americans but I don't like these white ones they've brought with them.' Since most, especially in the southern USA, experienced an inferior standard of living back home they did not constantly complain about the wartime conditions and lack of amenities in Britain. Official policy had it that no negroes were to be billeted out and they mostly lived in tents, with minimal facilities.

The palliative measures attempted by officialdom, both British and American, could not overcome the uneasiness felt by most people at the sight of a white woman with a black GI. Unfortunately, it was often young girls and the tartier women who actively pursued them, lured by money and the belief that they were better lovers. Marriage was out of the question. The US Army refused to ship white wives of black GIs to the USA, where such marriages were forbidden in many states. If a married woman strayed with a black man and had a child there was no disguising the fact of the liaison. Rumours went the rounds that the blacks were riddled with venereal disease. It was all a great propaganda gift to Goebbels, who lost no opportunity to taunt British servicemen overseas about the temptations presented by all the Americans – black and white – to the women they had left at home.

As American troops poured into the British Isles all the problems increased. There are stories of young girls besieging camps, prostitutes and enthusiastic amateurs entraining from the big cities or alternately flooding into the larger towns like bees to the honey pot. The *Bury St Edmunds Free Press* not infrequently reported instances of young girls up before the magistrates' court on charges of trespass. In March 1945 two women, who had come from Nottingham and Doncaster respectively, were arrested in an old ack-ack hut on an airfield, 100 yds from the airmen's quarters. They both swore that they had taken no money for their services, but they were made examples of and sentenced to one month in prison. The Provost Marshal said they usually just cautioned these women but the problem had become serious and there were far too many such instances of 'trespass'. Another case concerned a seventeen-year-old girl, already under supervision, who was undressed when found on the top bunk in the enlisted men's quarters; the time-honoured camp follower.

The London professionals, known as the 'Piccadilly Commandos' or 'Hyde Park Rangers', apparently were not the problem, being experienced in these matters and keeping to their own territory. Some areas of Mayfair were patrolled by French girls exclusively. In the West End around the Rainbow Club it was no holds barred, anything from £2 to £5 or even a pair of nylons. Much business was done in doorways, cheaper and quicker than hiring a room and often discreetly ignored by the patrolling constables. For many young, working class girls not old enough to be conscripted it was an opportunity to make money and have a bit of fun, work hard all day and go 'up west' in the evening. Lynford Hampton, briefly stationed at Bovingdon, writes, 'Piccadilly had an abundance of women soliciting for a pack of cigarettes or a £1. I viewed this as a struggle for survival, a fundamental fact of life.' It was not uncommon even in Wales for a GI 'to get propositioned six times in one evening. We never got over how easy it was to make it with the girls, and not just the single ones either.' From high to low apparently. When Eisenhower and Butcher were taking a stroll one evening in 1942 with a rather heavily built civilian friend they were approached by one of the ladies of the night who 'looked straight at George and said "Hallo, fat boy, does your mother know you're out?"'

When it came to venereal disease and unwanted pregnancies, sheer ignorance was often the problem. In the Britain of the 1940s VD, for example, was not a matter to be discussed in families. A young girl finding a condom thought it was a balloon, and, surprisingly, a fourteen-year-old boy confessed equal ignorance. It was mooted that by having sex in certain positions pregnancy was impossible. A thirteen-year-old in Wales was puzzled by some American soldiers coming up the road shouting 'Are there any dames in the houses we can sleep with?' Her mother explained it away by saying they were homesick for their mothers so wanted women to sleep with them! Above all, the intensive wooing of the GIs was to many women irresistible, perhaps most of all to women who had not seen their husbands for years. Inexperienced younger women were simply overwhelmed by the cornucopia of goodies that emanated from Uncle Sam. Not all though: Meg Thomas, working for the National Fire Service, was disgusted by one NCO who bragged he would go through every girl at the station before he was finished, and called Meg 'Frigid Bridget'. Inevitably, there were many wild exaggerations as to the numbers of pregnancies and incidents of VD. The rise in both was not entirely the responsibility of American servicemen. The Canadians could claim a large proportion of both, as could other assorted Allied servicemen, including the home team. The Poles had a certain reputation, as did the French, while Italian prisoners of war were rated the best lovers.

Attempts were made to combat VD and out came the Ministry of Information posters and in came 'prophylactic stations' at the larger ARC clubs. GIs were already issued with condoms and discarded ones littered the streets of cities and draped country hedgerows. Luckily penicillin made a very welcome appearance and a soldier was now *hors de combat* for weeks rather than months. Apparently, the incidence of VD was highest among bomber crews, both USAAF and RAF, who lived dangerously in every respect. There are obviously no statistics available for the number of back-street abortions carried out as a direct result of the 'friendly invasion' and the rise in illegitimate births is understandable in wartime. Babies were put up for adoption or incorporated into the family, possibly as a sister or brother. For the wives of servicemen abroad an unwanted pregnancy must have been a nightmare, although some husbands did accept the child, but rarely if it was black. Naturally, such a situation did not improve the long-term marital relationship.

If a GI did impregnate a girl the most obvious solution was marriage, but often that was a path strewn with obstacles. The GI could well be married already or promised elsewhere, or religion might be a stumbling block, particularly with Catholics and Jews. Sometimes the GI was willing but the girl's parents were not, and girls under twenty-one still needed parental consent. There were few 'quickie' weddings; the prospective bridegroom's Company Commander had to give his consent and often discouraged the man. A system evolved that included interviews, extensive form filling and a decent interval. A girl might deliberately get herself pregnant in order to catch herself a generous marriage allowance and a passport to paradise, the United States of America. If the senior officer suspected this he would have the man posted elsewhere.

There were some amusing incidents. A lady who had a lot of contact with the medical units says, 'Rumour had it that a US Medical Officer slept with his Scottish lady friend in the morgue at Aldermaston.' Years later this lady was falsely accused by an American wife of bearing her husband's child. She also says we have all since been presented with an edited version of events, women kept their secrets and, 'I somehow doubt if the Americans gave us a second thought as they sat on the verandah in their rocking chairs.'

There is much truth in the statement 'this edited version of events'. From the highest to the lowest in the hothouse atmosphere of wartime Britain, it took a lot of will power to resist entanglements, particularly for those working together on a daily basis. Kay Summersby Morgan did not write about her love affair with Gen Eisenhower until after his death. Yet it must have been common knowledge since, as his permanent driver, she was also his constant companion for almost three years. Drivers do not usually accompany their passengers to dine with Winston Churchill and the like. All the way down the line men and women would live for the day, the flier constantly aware that his next mission might be his last, the woman thinking she might not survive the next air raid or that her husband might be doing the same thing if he had the opportunity. The highest ranking staff officers could take their pick, for they had even more of whatever it took to attract the opposite sex, though that temptation was resisted by some. Harry Crosby turned down a staff appointment at USAAF Headquarters in Paris after spending a trial week at the Coty Mansion, where everything laid on was of superior quality, including the women. He elected to stay with the 100th BG 'where I was pretty sure I was good at what was expected of me'. The attraction of women 'Over There' caused much heartbreak for the wives and girlfriends of men, from whatever army, serving overseas.

It worked the other way too. John Costello spent an overnight pass in Southampton. He writes that he had avidly followed all news of the war and was well aware of conditions in Britain as a result of the Blitz and its 'social consequences'. He found a bed and breakfast: 'My room was bright and comfortable . . . it was so luxurious to slip between the sheets and pull the comforter up to my chin, after sharing close quarters in a tent on straw with six other GIs. I was awakened at dawn, the door being opened very carefully. My back was to the door, what do I do? Feign sleep? Then a young female appeared at the foot of the bed. Oh my God, it's true, their morals have slipped. No, they had not because the young person asked me "Will you take your tea (tay) in bed sir?" With that I was inaugurated into that pleasant British habit of having tea in bed, to get one's engine started for the day ahead.'

The root cause of many of the problems was indisputably drink. Alcohol-induced conviviality frequently led to lowered inhibitions and a consequent increase in confrontation, and not just confrontation between black and white GIs or locals and GIs, but between the different services. Harold Smith lived opposite the Mackworth Hotel in Swansea and remembers the tremendous street fights that frequently took place at closing time '[which] were usually between the American sailors and GIs. The US Navy Police sorted out the problem and they never pulled

John Costello of the 107th Separate Coast Artillery Battalion in 1943. (John Costello)

their punches. My sister and I used to sneak to the front window and watch every-thing from behind the curtains.' It was also drink that led to raucous behaviour on the streets. The British were very disapproving of the way some GIs would roam the streets, whisky bottle in hand, until spotted no doubt by the Snowdrops. The fact of being well away from home territory and unknown had a lot to do with it, as it still does. A Royal Navy rating ashore in Plymouth with his shipmates was approached by a rolling GI waving his whisky bottle, 'Hi Limeys do you wanna slug?' They finished the bottle. George Rosie says he got 'drunk and stupid' in Piccadilly staying on the street in an air raid and getting knocked flat in a bomb blast, then went on drinking. Even in the villages it was not so funny at closing time for the people living near a pub; there were many complaints about the noise after hours near airfields. An Oundle schoolboy remembers GIs wading into each other in the market place. They were usually fighting over female companions, or rather the lack of, in a town where every eligible girl could choose between several suitors. Getting drunk with a mate was probably the most common method of relaxation for any serviceman from whatever country, buying a drink for a stranger the best way to make a friend.

Something rarely mentioned in popular accounts of the Second World War was the number of men from all forces who suffered 'neuropsychiatric' (NP) problems. The Americans, by careful screening of draftees, had expected to weed out men who might be prone to such; it did not always work. John Costello tells of a member of his AA unit in 1942 at Tidworth who was 'homesick beyond anyone's comprehension'. His seven tent mates were aware of his depression, hid his 30-calibre ammunition and never left him alone. One day the GI watching him rushed off to the Mess hall without thinking, being late for lunch. 'He took about six steps when he heard a rifle roar within the tent. His buddy had sneaked one round of ammunition, and went home before any of us.' The problems, whatever they were, were exacerbated by the sheer numbers of Allied servicemen, mostly young and the majority American, jammed into the British Isles in extraordinary circumstances.

All things considered it could have been a lot worse.

CHAPTER 7

The Allies Interact

Much has been made of the resentment felt by British servicemen toward their American allies. They certainly had enough cause: the GIs looked better, were better paid, were enthusiastic in their pursuit of women and completely outnumbered the British armed forces on their own territory. An estimated 2 million US servicemen and women (though in truth very few women) passed through the British Isles during the Second World War. Following American entry into the war in December 1941, the first to arrive in strength were the 4,000 who stepped ashore in Northern Ireland. After that they just kept coming: 37,000 men moved through Ireland for the invasion of North Africa, Operation TORCH, in November 1942, 120,000 in preparation for D-Day; at the peak of the war there were 18 airfields in Northern Ireland for American use.

Apart from those initial encounters it was the airmen of the RAF and USAAF who were most likely to face each other when, from 1942, the 8th USAAF began to take over airfields in East Anglia. The RAF already knew and had mixed feelings about the American boys of the Eagle Squadrons. RAF airfields that were assigned to the Americans, however, always retained a British presence. It might be a maintenance unit or possibly a fire-fighting crew and frequently Air Traffic Control would stay in RAF hands, as might some administrative functions often carried out by WAAFs. The RAF kept an intelligence officer and manned the Post Office at Bassingbourn throughout the stay of the 91st BG.

Slightly wary at first, the RAF personnel thought the Americans too laid back, undisciplined and cocky, but soon came to appreciate the GI's capacity for hard work and willingness to adapt and learn. Those GIs who could acknowledge that the British experience of war did give them the right to teach and preach were obviously preferred to those who had little time for the British and their country. But all Americans knew something of the Battle of Britain and the heroism of the fighter pilots who unequivocally saved the British Isles from the terrifying experience of a German invasion. A few years later an RAF wife showed an ex-8th AF man a picture of her fighter pilot husband; he said he never forgot those 'wonderful guys'.

Publicity for Lend-Lease, photographed at Rhode Island. (US National Archives)

British pilots were helping to fly over American bombers, USAAF aircraft were controlled by RAF Air Traffic Control until the Americans were sufficiently trained and, in the early days, some RAF ground crew were seconded to help where the Americans were not fully geared up. Air Sea Rescue was an exclusively RAF operation, and many the crew of a ditched bomber had cause to be grateful. In June 1943 downed airmen of the 8th Air Force presented a cheque for £100 to Air Sea Rescue as a gesture of their appreciation. RAF fighters frequently escorted USAAF bombers to targets over Germany, especially in the early days of American participation. In 1943 air ace Wing Commander 'Johnny' Johnson was awarded the American Air Force Cross for just that service. Naturally, a sharp rivalry existed between the two services as is illustrated by this cleaned-up version of a well-known ditty:

The Yanks are flying Fortresses at 30,000 ft (repeated twice)
With bags of ammunition and a teeny weeny bomb

The RAF are flying Lancasters at zero zero ft (repeated twice)
With no ammunition and a bloody great bomb etc. etc.

Tom Winzor was in the RAF during the war and thought himself very fortunate to be working with Americans in a mixed section called No. 8 Special Liaison Unit. They were all trained in War Department cypher in St John's Wood and were then allocated to various operational Headquarters in the ETO:

Most units consisted of four officers (British or American) and eight senior RAF NCOs. It was my good fortune to be attached to HQ 8th US Bomber Command at Wycombe Abbey, where we lived in tents and worked under-ground. We received the same concessions as our friends the Yanks, we visited the PX where at around 4 p.m. daily we were able to buy cigarettes, candies, enjoy draught Coca-Cola on tap, and doughnuts. Our breakfasts usually consisted of four eggs and an equal number of rashers of bacon, plus a flapjack and syrup. I have never tasted better, it was gorgeous. The Americans were a lovely lot, I enjoyed two years with them, right up to the end of the war in Paris.

Being trained to fly in Georgia in 1941 alongside USAAF cadets proved to be an interesting and quite tough experience for Stanley Freestone. They were subjected to the West Point system of 'hazing', which means that any Upper Classman (in this case anyone who happened to be a mere five weeks ahead on the course) could bully those under him. Since everybody received the same treatment the RAF cadets had to put up with it, as they did the rather strange punishments imposed for misdemeanours.

Because we were in the deep south a white man could not be seen doing menial tasks. Thus no spud peeling but a system of de-merits . . . Everything at the

RAF aircrew cadets being entertained in Georgia, Alabama. Stanley Freestone (right) was one of the RAF aircrew undergoing training in the USA. (Stanley Freestone)

school was of first class quality. The food was wonderful if you ever had time to eat anything. The Upper Classmen were served first and the meal was finished when they decided to move off. Every moment of the duty day was timed to the minute, seldom leaving time to do anything except at the quickest possible speed . . . All the US servicemen I came across were patriotic and proud to be American; this pride was often misunderstood by the British who regarded it as an aggressive form of boasting. The next thing was their general friendliness and warmth. Although they had plenty to share with you they did in fact distribute with generosity.

On home ground RAF airmen who worked with the USAAF were very impressed with the Mess hall and 'huge steaks', and felt the Yanks lived much better. One aircraftman was very envious of the American uniform stores where a wide range of sizes were on offer. Another, from the care and maintenance party at a Wiltshire airfield, appreciated the much better rations and was very impressed by the fact that the American ground crew could afford to smoke large cigars. Don Earl was a Wireless Telegraphist at RAF Nutts Corner near Belfast who, when the Americans took over the base in 1942, stayed on with them for about three months. He most remembers 'the variety and abundance of food in the mess and the amount of goods, much of it free, at the PX. I was very sorry to return to austerity in Oxfordshire at the end of my secondment.' A corporal who worked with the Americans found them to be informal – 'could you do this for me bud?' – generous and kind. He was ashamed of the way the GIs were swindled in bars, etc., and was ashamed of the way our own servicemen would angle for free drinks from them – 'they've got plenty of money'. He did feel that many of the GIs, unsophisticated boys off the farms, could not hold their liquor. Working with an Intelligence Signals Unit adjacent to an American airfield at Parham in 1944, Bert Coulter, when off watch, used to go through the hedge and spend time with the B-17 ground crews. He was on hand when a B-17 crashed and caught fire. The men from his unit pulled out most of the aircrew from the blazing aircraft. 'Needless to say we later received a convivial response from the lower echelons on the base.'

The young WAAF clerk working in Sick Quarters at RAF Duxford was kept on when the Americans took over the station in April 1943. The Sick Quarters were at nearby Thriplow House. She comments, 'Discipline was quite different to ours; all very laid back, but in the long view efficient. They were kind, generous, loved children and, on the whole, a mixed bunch of very nice blokes a long, long way from home. Because I was young and unworldly they were particularly protective of me, and I never had any problems with them. Life was changed at Thriplow House, the food was different, a more relaxed atmosphere prevailed. We could always get a lift into Cambridge in one of the numerous jeeps and were allowed to use the PX – a very upmarket NAAFI!' Patricia Tester was a teleprinter operator with the Royal Corps of Signals, and also handled teletype traffic for the 82nd Airborne. Her contact was solely with the American signals staff, who were always 'well mannered and friendly'. She steered clear of the 'rougher' types who tried to pick her up in the streets and could be a nuisance. G. Hoar, a member of the Royal Observer Corps in Oxfordshire, says the post was often visited by American airmen based at Chalgrove 'who were very interested in our job and often came up for a cup of tea and a chat. They invited us to look around Chalgrove and while we were there a Fortress landed and we were taken aboard for a look round. The pilot then took us on a flight over the Thames Estuary; it was the highlight of my time in the ROC.'

There were neutral meeting grounds, such as a town hall in Wales which was open every day as a recreation centre for all Allied troops. Permanently in attendance were three American SPs and one British MP. A USAAF base 'somewhere in England' regularly entertained many groups, RAF and WAAF included. There were certainly official attempts to intermingle the disparate services. In one town 100 GIs were entertained at a British camp and then 100 British servicemen dined in an American Mess hall. The Anglo–American Army Relations Committee – reported in the *Stars and Stripes* – organised official exchanges of personnel consisting of one officer and ten men at a time. The GIs liked, among other things, the separate quarters and messes for NCOs; they thought it better for discipline and morale. They appreciated the authority of the British NCO; in the American services it was easier to 'make sergeant' and the NCOs often shared quarters with the men and addressed each other by their first names. The British addressed their NCOs by rank only. Most admired were the Regular Army NCOs, older, steadier, experienced men who properly looked after the men in their care. The GIs also preferred being waited on at table to the 'chow line' system of all US Messes. The Tommies were envious, obviously, of the better pay and conditions experienced by the GIs. Envious particularly of the constant supplies of hot water and cheap cigarettes, but did not care for the food as it was 'too rich'. They thought the GIs more self-assured and were amazed by the companionship between all ranks, consequent lack of discipline and the 'generosity

The Allies interact for coffee and donuts. (A.R. Coulter)

of all GIs'. The experience obviously changed preconceptions on both sides, 'I always thought the Americans were all blow and brag, I received a pleasant shock', and 'When one sees them at work one realises they are far from being the playboys they are thought to be.' Of their British counterparts the GIs said, 'Because of the British soldier's extreme politeness you would think he was a sissy, but he is far from that for he is a tough and rugged soldier. Overlook his accent and you'll discover a fine, lasting friend.' The Mississippi man still serving in the RAF in 1942 had only one complaint, 'They are so damn polite here. We Americans will come straight out and say "No you dumb bastard, you got an air filter not an oil filter". Here they mess about and say things like "Oh airman, you've got the wrong filter, pay attention."'

That was all good news, and when the British and Americans actually worked together or knew each other on a personal level a lot of the antagonism vaporised. Probably the first joint manoeuvres of Royal Marines and their American counterparts were held in South Wales in the autumn of 1942 in filthy weather, reports ex-Marine Bulgen. The newspaper account of the event quotes one of the US Marine officers as saying, 'Nobody knows how tough these Royal Marines are until he's trained with them a few months. I'd have just hated it like poison if we hadn't put on a pretty good show too.' These men were, of course, the cream of both services, all volunteers. The RNVR Lt Cdr Liaison Officer with an American Port Commando unit was less complimentary, scathing of the general lack of discipline and professionalism at all levels, and the immoderate standard of high living and entertainment lavished on the higher-ranking officers later in the war. However, he did find them nice individually. When US and RN ships tied up alongside each other in port the officers frequently entertained each other aboard: 'Our officers would take the booze aboard the "dry" American ships and come down the gangway afterwards with presents of food, fags and icecream.' The lower deck seemed to hit it off without any problems. Bert Gooch says his Royal Navy cruiser frequently tied up alongside American ships and 'gobs' and 'Jack Tars' went ashore together, the Americans ever generous with cigarettes and drinks. Sailors do seem to have been more tolerant of each other and minority groups generally.

Problems mostly arose when each was viewed en masse and from a distance. There was no denying the fact that at the lowest level the GI received almost four times the pay of a British private. Since Uncle Sam paid all living expenses the cash received on the 'day the eagle shits' was all funny money to be spent on entertainment, which mostly consisted of luring women away from the poor Tommy. Or so it seemed to the British soldier, or 'erk', in his rough, ill-fitting battledress, when ranged against the GI in his smooth gabardine walking-out uniform, throwing money at everything. The British serviceman in general, and particularly if he was serving overseas, resented the GI, for tales of sexual conquest and infidelity quickly spread. A British corporal with the 8th Army in Africa lost his fiancée to a US Lt Col – hardly surprising – and loathed all Americans thereafter.

The average GI, for his part, had little respect at first for his British counterpart, considering that he had no guts, had run away at Dunkirk, 'the Union Jack was red, white, blue and yellow', and put up with poor conditions and lousy pay. The British thought the GIs pampered, ill-disciplined and, of course, overpaid and unblooded. The latter was certainly the case initially, even Eisenhower had never been in a battle. The B-17 crews that arrived in August 1942 lacked training in formation flying, and could not take off, land or assemble in the dark. Dennis Bolam can remember B-17s limping home in the dusk, failing to maintain an orderly queue and wait for landing instructions. 'I'm coming in Bud' was the often-heard cry. This limited their actions over the continent to a short, daylight period which, until the P51s were available as escort, meant they were easy prey for German fighters. The 8th AF was, however, to be 'blooded' quickly enough.

At staff level cooperation was ongoing; the professionals on both sides knew better than to let personal grudges or dislikes get in the way of the business of war. Before the USA's entry into the war the exchanges of high-powered military delegations ensured that by the time of the attack on Pearl Harbor many were already acquainted, if not always in total agreement. Gen Dwight D. Eisenhower's appointment as Supreme Commander Allied Expeditionary Forces in December 1943 was a surprising choice. Gen Sir Alan Brooke, Chief of the Imperial General Staff, who had expected to get the job, had his reservations. He considered that Eisenhower was a coordinator rather than a strategist, but 'a good mixer, a champion of inter-Allied co-operation, and in those respects few can hold a candle to him'. Roosevelt and Churchill knew the job needed a politician as much as a tactician. Churchill had said of Gen Eisenhower, 'one of the finest men I have ever met', and both he and President Roosevelt were aware of the admiration and affection felt by the British officers who had worked with him. Lord Louis Mountbatten, appointed Chief of Combined Operations, hit it off particularly well with Eisenhower and they shared the same attitudes. Gen Marshall 'liked Mountbatten from the start', very useful for Combined Operations. Marshall was less enthusiastic about Alan Brooke, finding him 'icy and condescending', but did respect the man. Robert Sherwood quotes Eisenhower's remark to the very anti-British (and anti-everybody) Gen George S. Patton, 'I don't mind if one officer refers to another as that son of a bitch. But the instant I hear of any American referring to a brother officer as that <u>British</u> son of a bitch, out he goes.' Patton's feeling towards the British got worse rather than better when they crossed swords in North Africa. The divisions of command between the Allies could have proved a nightmare and it was often uneasy. Eisenhower, though frequently 'boiling with rage', says Kay Summersby, even managed to avoid open hostilities with Gen Bernard Montgomery, appointed Commander-in-Chief Allied Ground Forces for the initial phase of Overlord. Monty, however, was quite complimentary about them: 'of the American soldier I was not so sure – however I need have had no fear'. Eisenhower's aide, Capt Butcher, writes that when he first came to England he held all the usual prejudices but had found that beneath the seemingly cold Englishman's exterior is a 'warmth and sense of humour in which I find a particular delight'.

That Yank in Bomber Command, Robert Raymond, gives some interesting opinions on inter-service relationships from the inside. His opinion of his fellow rankers in the RAF in December 1940: 'In fact, Englishmen, the majority of the working class, have very little initiative. Instead they devote their minds to, and misplace their energies in, grumbling. The officers and commissioned personnel in general were the finest type of men, but the ranks have been held down too long.' He often mentions and is scathing of the British class system, the old school tie syndrome, which he considered prevented those without the 'right' accents getting commissions. With him on the course, when he was sent to continue flying training at Brize Norton in January 1942, were some fellow Americans: 'All of them are unanimous in their dislike of this country. To them the bread tastes like sawdust, they can't get a "cuppa cawfee"; . . . Above all they dislike RAF officers and take few pains to disguise their feelings.' When the first US officers appeared in their smart pink pants his RAF comrades jeered 'Looks like a bloody ballet line' but Raymond was impressed with the Americans' generally smart appearance, even if they did 'look a bit like ushers at the Roxy'. Raymond, like most of the Americans who served initially in the RAF, found the transfer to the USAAF strange and quite difficult. He had forgotten what his fellow citizens were like, 'having been too long used to the more class-conscious British way. The Yankee energy displayed here is infectious. It makes me feel I've been sleepwalking. But with this kind of food it's no wonder that they can maintain that pace.'

It is estimated that 50 per cent of the wartime GI brides were members of the armed forces or Land Girls, so it is a fair assumption that the women's services got on well with the American servicemen. The Americans were very impressed by them. Gen Raymond Lee, taken on a tour of inspection in 1941, was called for by a WAAF driver: 'these girls are extremely well-disciplined, they clean their own cars, open the doors, salute, close the doors, keep their mouths shut and respectfully decline to have any meals or tea with their passengers, no matter who they are.' Not entirely, there was the previously mentioned famous attachment between driver and passenger. American pilots were often talked down by WAAF ATC, much admired for their quiet, calm efficiency and lovely voices, and Americans who came across servicewomen in an official capacity were very appreciative of 'these hardworking, courageous girls'.

Women in uniform are as attractive to men as the converse. Most of the girls loved the way the Americans behaved towards them and were attracted, in the usual way, to alien charms. The wedding of a WAC to a British soldier in North Africa took place in July 1943, so it worked both ways. The WAAFs were probably in the closest proximity, sometimes sharing an airfield, many were 'bowled over' but other girls, although finding the Americans 'very polite', preferred to socialise with the RAF men. A girl in the ATS, posted to a village in Wiltshire, arrived the day after tank units of Gen Patton's 3rd Armoured Division moved in prior to D-Day. 'They were the tops, couldn't fault them . . . we used to have their PX rations, gum and cigarettes, we spent some lovely evenings with them in their canteen and at concerts, wonderful men, no complaints whatsoever'.

How did the American servicewomen get on with their British counterparts? It is doubtful that their paths crossed very often since the WACs and WAVES were decidedly thin on the ground. The *Stars and Stripes* reports in December 1943 that 150 WACs hosted a tea party for British and Canadian servicewomen. Camilla Mays Frank, a WAC Special Services officer, worked at the top level with British servicewomen and got on well with them.

So where was the trouble? It erupted, if anywhere, at the pub, and probably at closing time when the younger and less inhibited patrons tended to spill out noisily shouting the odds. Sometimes a specific incident would spark it off: as previously mentioned, British servicemen being unhappy with the situation between white and black GIs, or just a deliberately provocative remark. It did not take much when both sides were tanked up and with real or imagined grievances, often over women (see the poem below), but just as often in fierce defence of a friend, unit, army, leader or nation.

The following extract from a poem was found by his sister among the effects of a Cambridge man.

Oh Mother this Cambridge is a horrible sight
with the Yanks gadding around it
by day and by night
These 'ere Cambridge women
Don't arf make you think
They would auction their souls
for the price of a drink

The chumps of the States
Oh so cocky and bold
Are having their fun here
and paying in gold
The women flock round them
The money goes fast
And the chumps think their charms
have been noticed at last

They come into town
and look over the herd
They pick out a sitter
perhaps some guy's wife
Very soon she is hog-tied
and branded for life

And in the midst of this barter and vice
I've found a young lady
who really is nice
In prayer to my maker I always give thanks
That there is one girl at least
Who's not crazy on Yanks.

CHAPTER 8

D-Day and Beyond

The huge build-up of American troops in Britain – more than 1½ million by June 1944 – was the culmination of years of planning. The invasion of continental Europe, codenamed Overlord, was at last given the go-ahead for June 1944. The High Command had agreed its final plan and, to confuse enemy intelligence, Gen Patton's phantom army was supposedly assembled in the south-east of England, aimed at the Pas de Calais. In March Eisenhower's SHAEF Headquarters had moved out of Grosvenor Square to Widewing, Bushy Park, near Richmond. Gen Eisenhower had been named as Supreme Commander in December 1943. There were some mutterings; the British resented an American being at the top and the Americans resented the fact that all Eisenhower's immediate deputies were British. Deputy Supreme Commander was ACM Sir Arthur Tedder, Adm Sir Bertram Ramsey was to be in charge of naval operations and the air job went to ACM Leigh Mallory. Gen Sir Bernard Montgomery ('whose talent for fighting the Germans was only equalled by his ability to infuriate the Americans from Eisenhower down', wrote Harold Macmillan) was given command of initial land forces. Eisenhower proved his worth many times over, placating, cajoling, ordering and threatening this Anglo-American conglomeration of top brass. A master of compromise, he decreed that coffee should be served in the morning and tea in the afternoon. Harold Nicolson was to write on 30 July that cooperation in Normandy 'has been quite splendid. It is very much due to Eisenhower's personal tact and charm.'

These oast houses at Staplehurst became offices for the 363rd Fighter Group prior to D-Day. (Kent Messenger)

Snowdrops on duty at Staplehurst. (*Kent Messenger*)

Most of the divisions of infantry scheduled to take part in Overlord spent only a short time in Britain. The 1st Infantry Division, known as 'The Big Red One', 'all piss and vinegar', was brought back from North Africa because the Americans had so few men experienced in battle. The training was intensive, recalls Jules Honig of the 294th Combat Engineers, 4th Division:

[arriving at a] typical country estate which had been modified to function as an engineer training camp. The commander was a full colonel and he was there to break our backs – not a funny man at all. One incident happened after a 12 mile combat simulation. We went out in full combat gear and after a weird night of groping in the dark we returned to base at 4 a.m. to find him waiting to review us. He didn't like the way we looked and ordered us back out to repeat the same exercise . . . The pre-invasion training was rigorous, but at age 19 my pool of energy seemed limitless. On June 1st all training stopped abruptly and we were moved to a staging area near Weymouth. We all knew that the invasion was near. The food quality improved 100%. No more green powdered eggs for breakfast, or corned beef hash for dinner. Now we had fresh eggs with sausages, and whole milk for breakfast, and steak with French fries and ice cream for dinner. One could hear it said everywhere 'This is the big feed-up for the kill.'

On the march in Britain just before D-Day. (IWM AP25496)

George Rosie with the 101st Airborne talks of 25-mile hikes, six days a week, in full equipment and carrying machine-guns or 44-lb mortars, which had predictable results: 'men passed out'. They continued practice jumps, including a demonstration for Winston Churchill and Gen Eisenhower – which was not without accidents – and did an exchange with the British 6th Airborne.

The most infamous training exercise was Tiger, held at Slapton Sands in South Devon. Concerned about the inexperience of most men, both Army and Navy, Eisenhower decreed that live ammunition would be used for this series of battle simulations but the men were not to be told. The landings made on the morning of 27 April 1944 by Force U destined for Utah Beach were witnessed by the Supreme Commander Eisenhower himself, ACM Tedder and Gen Omar Bradley, commander of the American 1st Army. There were many hitches and the C-in-C and his party, who left that evening, were not impressed. They therefore missed the second wave of eight Landing Ship Tanks (LST), ostensibly escorted by two destroyers, except that one had returned to port with mechanical problems. There was a breakdown of radio communication and the LST commanders did not receive a warning message reporting German E-Boats in the area. The nine E-Boats were on standard reconnaissance from Cherbourg and could not believe their eyes when they spotted the LSTs apparently unescorted. What happened afterwards is common knowledge now, thanks to Ken Small who, after extensive research, lists 638 US Army and Navy men dead and missing, more than the total at Utah on D-Day itself.

As far as possible the soldiers assembling for D-Day were grouped as for the beach-heads, the US 1st Army to the west, the 29th Division near Plymouth, the 4th Infantry in the Dartmouth area and the British and Canadian armies gathered in the south-east. Their disposition was a miracle of organisation; pouring a quart into the pint pot that was this small island. The British, says Lt Downing of the 1st Division, were getting edgy: 'There were signs they were becoming testy about being crowded out of their pubs, their buses and their cinemas and having their girls monopolised by Americans.' The troops were jammed in everywhere and

The infantry prepares for D-Day. (US National Archives)

Troops come ashore on the South Devon coast during a rehearsal for D-Day. (IWM EA21843)

bedded down in old schools, empty houses, deserted barracks and factories, in tents, in forests and fields, and in staging areas surrounded by barbed wire.

Situated in a small village on the Somerset–Devon border, a farmer had to have a pass to move about his own farm: 'In one of our fields a group of D-Day men were stationed and well guarded.' These men were from an airborne unit to be dropped by the 94th Troop Carrier Squadron. When they moved out during the night nobody heard anything. Young Joe Duggan's adopted gun crew were confined to barracks from the beginning of June, 'they handed in their walking-out uniforms and covered their AA guns in thick grease. Little did I realise as I left their quarters on June 5th that the next day they would all be gone.' In Broadmayne near Dorchester, prior to D-Day, three camps were established in and around the village and the GIs organised dances and socials in the village hall. 'The last memory I have of the Americans was when they were all moving out for the invasion, hundreds of lorries filled with men filed past us as we were walking home from the shops. As we waved them goodbye they threw out money to us saying they wouldn't need it where they were going.' This happened frequently: 'when they left for France they gave my children lots of ball games and English money which helped us as we did not earn much'.

The reverse side of the coin, literally, happened to one fifteen-year-old lad when he encountered a very disconsolate GI sitting alone on a doorstep: 'I asked him why, and he said he was broke and couldn't join his pals who were having a last night out. I, having saved the great sum of 15 shillings, a lot of money in those days to a fifteen-year-old, gave it to this Yank. He of course promised to pay me back. I feel I helped in some small way.' 'There they were lined along the roadside, mile after mile in either direction, as far as the eye could see. Every truck load handing us sweets and still asking if we had any older sisters at home.' Near Southampton the troops took over the clubhouse of a bowls club: 'Many side roads were lined with trucks, Jeeps, every type of vehicle, covered with camouflage netting. And then one morning they were all gone – the streets completely empty – it must have been about June 4th.' 'During the build-up to the invasion US Army lorries

Tanks practise landings. (US National Archives)

were parked along the Western Esplanade, Southampton, with the troops living aboard. Father used to let them come in and get washed, boil water for coffee etc. A week or two later the swimming baths on the Esplanade were used to coffin the bodies as they were brought back from France and put on transport ships home.'

In Swansea Pamela Thomas' family had a brief encounter with some American servicemen:

. . . it was one Sunday lunchtime in 1944 when there was a commotion in our street. When we went to investigate, we saw lots of American soldiers sitting on the kerbside with their kitbags. A policeman approached my father and asked if we would billet two of these men. We were a family of four living in a three bedroom house (two bedrooms and a boxroom). My brother and I shared the boxroom so that the Americans could have the larger bedroom. Hugh Ward from New Jersey and Arthur Savoy from Coney Island joined

One of the assembly areas for D-Day, which the cows do not seem to mind sharing. (IWM OWIL29920)

Waving goodbye to their friends. (IWM EA9009)

our family . . . one day the 'boys' came home and told us they were moving to an unknown destination, but we knew it was something big. A dance and buffet was put on in the local school as a farewell gesture. The following evening all the families who had taken in the American boys congregated at the Cottage Homes, where we said our tearful goodbyes and the convoy of lorries moved out. We didn't know at the time but they were taking part in the D-Day landings and were presumably going to Swansea Docks to board ship. However, the next day we all had a wonderful surprise, as they all returned due to D-Day being postponed. Unfortunately we had to go through the 'goodbyes' all over again.

It would seem that even when GIs were only briefly stationed in an area cordial and lasting relationships were established.

For those who had formed attachments over a long period the parting was deeply upsetting. 'Life was never the same again. Gone were the doughnuts and the candy, and gone were the long lines of jeeps, tanks and DUKWs that always seemed to be parked on the streets. We had nothing to climb on anymore and we would never see the like of it again.' Joe Duggan at Buckfastleigh never forgot 6 June 1944, when at about 2 a.m. 'there was bedlam, the whole battery was paraded in the car park. I hung out of my bedroom window crying like mad. Then they were gone, leaving a great emptiness in my life.' Having been confined to camp for days the men had no opportunity to bid their British girlfriends farewell and messages were left in the abandoned camps.

Alas many of these girls never heard from their GIs again, for if they became casualties only the next of kin were notified and if not, they had probably moved on to pastures new. As the American soldiers left their British friends behind they must have been very apprehensive. Few had been in action before, with notable exceptions being the 1st and 9th Infantry Divisions, and in spite of the hectic few weeks or months of training running up to June 1944, they were still untried. The Wehrmacht had a formidable reputation and therefore the invasion was not going to be a walkover.

The mountain of supplies needed to maintain the lifestyle the GIs were accustomed to was

Lt Willis H. Kennedy Jr of the 91st BG ready for take-off, 1944. (US National Archives)

Above: Loading blankets at a supply depot as part of the preparations for D-Day. (IWM D17020)

Right: Build up for D-Day as the ammunition goes on board. (IWM AP42798)

prodigious and took up valuable shipping space. According to Max Hastings, the initial American force of 130,000 would take with it some 140,000 vehicles. More significantly, it was planned that every American soldier in Normandy would receive 6¼ lbs of rations daily as against the German soldier's 3⅓ lbs. The logistics for backing up the American invasion force alone was an enormous undertaking, requiring as the men put it, 'one man in the line and six to bring up the Coca-Cola'. The equipment, consisting of more than thirty items, each paratrooper was to carry about his person proved to be so heavy and awkward that many men were drowned when they were dropped by error over water. British senior officers still had their doubts as to the quality of the American junior officers, as did Capt Harry Butcher after witnessing Exercise Tiger in April: 'I am concerned over the absence of toughness and alertness of young American officers whom I saw on this trip. They seem to regard the war as one grand maneuver in which they are having a happy time. Many seem as green as growing corn. How will they act in battle, and how will they look in three months' time? A good many of the full colonels also give me a pain. They are fat, grey and oldish. Most of them wear the Rainbow Ribbon of the last war and are still fighting it.'

Planning for D-Day had been ongoing since 1942; the proposal for an artificial harbour had first been suggested by Adm Mountbatten in the spring of 1942. The idea of an engineer called Guy Mansell, it greatly appealed to Churchill and was later implemented. The construction of the Mulberry harbour, and PLUTO, the oil pipeline under the ocean, were truly amazing undertakings which were apparently never spotted by German intelligence. The Mulberry harbour alone required a labour force of 45,000 men, and the information could so easily have been leaked. Work did not begin until December 1943, so it was always a race against time. However, it was done, and in the spring of 1944 a tug called *The Empire Derby* left Liverpool for a more northern port. Mollie Warner's husband was aboard the tug at the time and she relates the story:

A bomb dump in a Kent wood. (Kent Messenger)

Loading a Landing Ship Tank (LST). (By courtesy of *The News*, Portsmouth)

A mobile textile repair shop. (By courtesy of *The News*, Portsmouth)

On arrival they took in tow a huge section of Mulberry Harbour, were fitted with a barrage balloon and sailed south. The tug carried a crew of some ten men, and a machine-gun complete with a Royal Navy gunner. The boat was based in Southampton Docks, where its job was to tow landing craft out to sea and berth troop ships. One day when most of the crew were officially off duty the gunner stripped and cleaned the gun, some of the crew giving him a hand. When it was fully assembled the gunner sat back for a smoke and one of the deckhands started playing with the gun. Moored nearby was an American troopship with American troops lining the rails. The deckhand, still playing around with the gun, aimed it at the troopship and said 'Bang, bang' not realising that the ammo belt was loaded and in firing mode. With the result that a number of Americans were shot in the legs. An inquiry was held and the deckhand was cleared of malicious intent. I often wonder if those US troops on Veterans' Day parades, proudly wearing their Purple Hearts, ever mentioned that they never did cross the Channel.

But on that dramatic morning of 6 June 1944 Allied troops did cross the Channel, transported and protected by 600 warships and under the umbrella cover of thousands of friendly aircraft. Casualties were actually being treated in hospitals in Britain by 11.30 p.m. that same day. The big invasion ports of Portsmouth and Southampton were receiving both Allied wounded and German prisoners of war the very next day. The ships who had taken out the invasion forces were now homeward bound with casualties on board. The big naval hospitals at the ports were used as reception centres, hospital trains at the ready to remove wounded on to hospitals in the south-east. American servicemen would be transferred to their own hospitals and shipped home as soon as it was possible, more than 10,000 American nurses having been brought over in anticipation. Casualties there were in plenty; 2,000 that first day on Omaha Beach alone, so vividly simulated in films since. It all went badly wrong on Omaha, and the 82nd Airborne suffered heavy casualties at St Mère Eglise, but first-day objectives were achieved, and follow-up units began to come ashore. Within 24 hours 176,000 troops were ashore and it was, in Churchill's words, the 'beginning of the end'.

The troops embark for Operation Overlord. (US National Archives)

The Troop Carrier Command 9th Air Force C-47s used for the airborne drops picked up wounded for the return journey, as tactical units of the 9th continued shooting up the German communications and providing cover for the troopships. The US 9th Air Force was a very movable feast and squadrons had briefly transferred to other airfields for the D-Day operation: 'We'd spent the nights before the landings into France painting black and white stripes on our A-20s.' Air Groups moved to the continent to support the armies as soon as suitable landing strips became available, the units remaining in Britain were kept busy ferrying supplies to the advancing troops. Although only 130,000 GIs went in on that first wave on 6 June (British and Canadian troops actually outnumbered the Americans), the gaps were immediately noticeable in London. On 12 June Mollie Panter-Downes writes, 'There's lots more room on the pavements for one thing, now that the uniforms, both British and American, have thinned out . . . civilians lifting a

A roadside canteen. (By courtesy of *The News*, Portsmouth)

Roadside lunch while waiting to embark for D-Day. (By courtesy of *The News*, Portsmouth)

timid finger for a taxi are overwhelmed when 2 or 3 attentive cabbies race up'. In September SHAEF Headquarters moved to France, but large numbers of American troops still passed through the British Isles en route to France, and upwards of 100,000 were recuperating in British hospitals at any one time in the months that followed.

D-Day did mark the turning point in most respects: billets were turned back to the owners, training grounds cleared and many of the tensions felt by both the GIs and the host nation were eased if not alleviated. GIs spending their leaves in Britain tended to be more appreciative of the country after having had a taste of action. There is a letter in the *Stars and Stripes* from a 2nd lieutenant in hospital

Gen Eisenhower talks to men of the 101st Airborne. (IWM EA25491)

A game of cards for the men of a Divisional HQ Company awaiting shipment. (By courtesy of *The News*, Portsmouth)

who says he is sick and tired of published letters 'ridiculing the British' and praises the guts and character shown by British civilians and soldiers. GIs were to have a taste of a different kind of action, particularly if they stayed in London. On the night of 12 June 1944 Hitler launched his secret weapon, the unmanned Vergeltungswaffe 1 (V1), against the capital. Stan Kieffer made a trip to London at about this time:

> Just after checking in at a Red Cross club the air-raid siren went off. In the darkness we could see the searchlights trying to pick out the night raiders. Suddenly I could hear the Buzz Bomb and saw the tail glow. The bomb made a noise like a washing machine. Suddenly the noise stopped and we heard an explosion. After a sleepless night I went to Piccadilly Circus, and while talking to a friendly policeman found out the bomb had landed just a few streets away and had hit a WAAF barracks, killing 12 girls. Decided then and there to cancel my weekend in London and did not go back until the war was over.

Families at home in the USA now had even more cause to worry about their menfolk, and with good reason; by the end of that first month 1,935 civilians had been killed and over 5,000 wounded. In July four WACs were injured, and later some GIs were killed by V1s, while 3,000 US engineers were assigned to help clear bomb damage in London.

The positive side of the fighting in Normandy was that the British and American soldiers now had a great deal more in common. An infantryman is an infantryman, and the same horrors were experienced by them all; nobody was unblooded after Normandy. Harold Nicolson writes to his sons on 30 July after lecturing to American troops: 'They all agree that British and American troops *always* get on badly when they just glower at each other in the streets and *always* get on well when they have a joint job to do.' In the months that followed only the 8th Air Force remained predominantly on the British side of the Channel; as the front moved east in Europe many of the back-up units transferred to the continent and the GIs had started their exodus.

From the British Isles the 8th Air Force Bomb Groups, protected by their fighters, continued to pound targets in continental Europe. Troop Carrier Groups made further drops of men and supplies. From Ramsbury on 17 September 1944 the 437th TCG put up seventy aircraft and gliders carrying units of the 101st Airborne for Operation Market Garden, Montgomery's plan to establish a bridgehead across the Rhine. On the Group's worst day ever they lost eight aircraft. In December they dropped supplies to the trapped 101st Airborne at Bastogne, but on 25 February 1945 all the aircraft of the 437th left Ramsbury

The 2nd Air Division bids a final farewell somewhere in Norfolk, 1945. (IWM EA2996)

for a base some 20 miles east of Paris. The RAF was to take over the airfield a month after VE Day. This pattern was repeated all over. The 78th FG of the 66th Fighter Wing at Duxford flew its final mission on 25 April and the countdown to departure began. On August Bank Holiday they held a big open day and visitors queued to climb into the P51 Mustangs. The 93rd BG at Hardwick also flew its last mission on 25 April, the group's 391st. The planes were flown back to the USA while the ground crews, scheduled to move on to the war in the Pacific, went home on the *Queen Mary*. The 66th Wing Headquarters Squadron at Sawston was also intended for the Pacific theatre without any home leave en route.

In the euphoria following VE Day, although the war was not yet over, there were celebrations in plenty. USAAF airfields played host to their hosts, and in Cambridge the 8th Air Force was given the freedom of the city. Thanking the mayor, Gen William E. Kepner, Commander of the 2nd Air Division, said, 'What you are doing for us today is but a further manifestation of the kindness, the helpfulness and the friendship the people of Cambridge have shown us since our arrival in England three years ago. We have a feeling that we have been Freemen

Celebrating the alliance. (US National Archives)

of the Borough of Cambridge, unofficially, ever since the first Eighth Air Force member came to town as a sightseer.' Earlier on 31 July there had been a Farewell America Ball at the Guildhall. In Sawston, on 25 August when the war was truly over, there was a grand Anglo-American fête. Three days later the 312th Signal Company held open house, and by the end of October they were all gone. Little did everybody know as they bade their tearful farewells that within three years the USAAF would be back to prepare to face a new enemy.

But as the GI presence dwindled away, from 400,000 in May down to 62,000 by November 1945, there were those who breathed a sigh of relief. Farmers might recover their land, owners their requisitioned properties and British men their women. Some felt that 'the Americans left in a blaze of ill feeling' not least because of the enormous and offensive waste of food and all those things that were in desperately short supply in Britain. Burnt or crushed by the bulldozer; the paperwork required to hand these items over would have been too complicated.

CHAPTER 9

Consequences

D-Day had marked the high noon of the American occupation of Britain and, as Allied forces slowly pushed back the German Army, the sense of all pulling together somehow began to dissipate, especially on the political front. The anti-British lobby in the USA, never quiet for long, again reared its head: why should the USA fight on to sustain that anachonism, the British Empire? Those 'civilians in uniform', the GIs, became increasingly anxious to be civilians again, especially after the horrors of physically engaging the enemy. The experience of serving overseas had all kinds of long-term consequences, and one of the most significant was that so many young men in the prime of life got themselves a foreign bride.

Marrying a GI was not that simple. The American hierarchy was anxious to shield their men from hasty, ill-conceived relationships, and equally concerned not to antagonise the folks back home. There certainly were coercive pregnancies; sometimes the soldier was already spoken for or even already married, without the knowledge of his British fiancée. It was particularly the fathers of the girls who objected to their daughters marrying Yanks, for with it went all the connotations: she was 'easy pickings' or could not get herself a decent British husband. Nor did he want his daughter to live thousands of miles away. To generalise is dangerous, as some parents were enchanted by the young man their daughter brought home. They made no objections to the marriage, pleased that their child would have a chance for a better, brighter future. Girls under twenty-one in any case needed parental consent. In the fevered atmosphere running up to D-Day there were many hasty engagements, and sometimes that was the last the girl heard from her erstwhile fiancé. Equally, many GIs were determined to take home a British bride, attracted by the cultural differences. British girls were said to be less demanding than American girls, had better complexions and were more quietly spoken and less assertive.

Whatever the reason, 70,000 British girls were wed to American servicemen in the period 1942–6 (estimates vary, but most settle on this figure), and of these brides apparently 50 per cent came from the women's services. To keep it in context let us not forget that 12,000 GIs married Australian girls and 40,000 British girls married Canadians: the consequence of letting loose vast numbers of young men away from their home environment. These brides would soon have to adapt to their new country, and the sooner they began the better. The club at Rainbow Corner organised classes and fashion shows for GI brides and brides-to-be. Instruction was given on how to dress, how to make up and how to behave, especially with in-laws. They were advised to be smartly dressed and wear lipstick for that first interview with the husband's family. The problems had only just begun for the girls who did manage to overcome family opposition on both sides of the Atlantic. Not just the girls, as there were quite a few weddings between American girls and British servicemen. They married aircrew in Tulsa, sailors in New York and some even managed to get over to Britain to marry. Olwen Evans' brother, Frank, married an American girl in Britain during the war: 'They had met when Frank and his twin brother were sent to the USA on a mission by the War Office, to do with Radar.'

When the war ended the wounded and repatriated prisoners of war were naturally given first priority on west-bound ships. They were followed by GIs, rated on a points system. Brides had to obtain an affidavit of support from

GI bride-to-be Dorothy Sole with fiancé Cpl Bob Christman of the 91st BG. (Vince Hemmings)

Operation GI Bride gets under way; the first shipment sails away on SS Argentina, *26 January 1946. The exercise began after an Act was passed in congress allowing the brides exemption from the 'Immigration Quota'.* (IWM HU36289)

their husbands as they awaited transport and, at this point, some unfortunates discovered they were being divorced. Once back on home territory the spouse had second thoughts, or was talked out of his wartime alliance. It was not until January 1946 that the first shipment of GI brides got under way after an Act of Congress, passed in December 1945, gave foreign brides exemption from the immigration quota. The brides had first to spend a few days at a reception centre, for processing and a medical, and therein lie a few horror stories. Some girls recall nothing, 'it was all a blur', while others remember the shaming medical, or some of the women who 'made it' with staff GIs or the German prisoner of war orderlies. For they were a very mixed crowd indeed. Even at this first hurdle some girls got cold feet and went home to mother, and who can blame them? One girl got to Southampton with her baby to find her ship delayed with mechanical problems. Her family, always reluctant to let her go, persuaded her to not go at all.

Staff Sgt Stan Kieffer and his bride, January 1946. (Judith Kieffer)

For those who did set sail to the New World the journey was no ocean cruise. The crossing in February 1946 on the *Zebulin B. Vance*, a converted liberty ship, took fourteen awful days for Hilda Graham and her small baby. Everybody was seasick, the babies were ill and when the ship arrived in New York it was quarantined for two days. Hilda lost 18 lbs in weight on the voyage. On one infamous trip across ten babies were reported to have died. Conditions on most ships did improve with time and experience and later travellers had medical staff in attendance, the correct baby foods and even, miraculously, disposable diapers. The arrival in New York could be equally traumatic. Because there had been instances of women disappearing ashore on arrival, their sham marriages a ticket to paradise, the immigration officials at New York in those days tended to be aggressive and hardly welcoming. Intent on keeping out 'illegals', they reduced some girls to tears in the alien surroundings: 'they demanded payment of duty on wedding presents, I had no dollars and had to beg and borrow from a fellow passenger until I could contact my husband outside the barrier. I could have stayed there all day for all they cared.' Betty Kieffer sailed across in June 1946, by which time all the arrangements had been perfected. She was kept on board ship for three days after arrival for intensive screening, and to give the American Red Cross time to arrange onward journeys, the general policy by then being to discourage the eager bridegrooms from descending on New York. 'The Red Cross did a marvellous job, paying the fare and escorting the groups of girls to various destinations. On the train one girl given corn on the cob tried to cut it with her knife and fork!'

As well as having to go through the ordeal of meeting in-laws the girls had frequently to adjust to the vagaries of an unfamiliar climate. 'On arrival in Minneapolis in intense heat, after all the stress of the past few weeks, all I wanted to do was sleep. I heard my mother-in-law telling somebody on the phone how lazy I was.' Another girl arrived in Texas in August wearing clothes suitable for a British winter. She was unable to eat properly for weeks. Even for the girls who got a warm welcome it was a cultural shock. The myriad bright lights were a physical shock after years of black-out, the mountains of food disconcerting. 'I went to my sister-in-law's family farm where they had the largest dining table I have ever seen and it was loaded with all kinds of foods, meat, vegetables, bread, cakes, pies, and they expected me to eat some of all of it.' Betty Kieffer recalls, 'I always remember my first meal in a restaurant. Trays of half eaten steak, a whole week's ration, being returned to the kitchen.' Like so many others of her generation, Betty never became accustomed to the horrendous waste of everything, including energy. In a Minnesota winter with outside temperatures often below zero, houses and stores were kept at 75° to 80° Fahrenheit: 'I was amazed to see women wearing cotton summer dresses inside their homes in winter, while outside there were four foot snowdrifts.'

In addition to adapting to a new country and a new family the GI bride had to adjust to a new husband. For the man who met her off the train or boat was not the dashing man in uniform she had married. Civilian men wore wide-brimmed trilby hats, wide-shouldered loose-fitting suits and – to British eyes – garish ties. Some brides actually failed to recognise their husbands. Gone was the devil-may-care laughing boy, instead a man who might not have a job, almost certainly had nowhere of his own to live, and was having his own problems of adjustment. Who was this man? Some girls were barely acquainted with their new spouses, one GI bride had only actually met her husband eleven times in all, although having known him for thirteen months prior to the marriage.

How welcome this new daughter-in-law was made depended very much on the ethnic background of the family. One girl's in-laws were both born in Italy, 'I did have a job adjusting to the Italian way of life, not to the American', but was warmly welcomed into a large, noisy family. Another, after all this time, remains firmly British, being fortunate enough to have a British-born mother-in-law, her husband's grandparents still living in Britain. A bride might find herself in a rigidly German enclave with set patterns of behaviour. Some drew the short straw; one girl flew over at her own expense to wed the soldier she loved, only to find him mentally and physically changed after being wounded in France. They lived in a cabin built on the family farm and she always had to work. For girls used to city life the most difficult adjustment was to life on a farm, perhaps miles from anywhere.

Most started married life sharing a house with in-laws, which is never an ideal situation. The new bride was introduced to strange combinations of food, 'pure white bread brought me out in a rash', as well as rigid religious and social structures. In the environment in which one bride found herself ladies always carried a 'purse' (handbag) to match their shoes, and on certain occasions the hat had to match as well. The liberally educated girl from Edinburgh, accustomed to moving in many circles, found she was restricted to a single coterie, and expected to talk only to other women. Also difficult to assimilate was the sheer noise level generated by a nation of apparent extroverts. On the credit side the hospitality extended to these foreign brides was usually warm and well meaning, if overwhelming. One young bride taking her first overnight train journey to a new life was escorted and treated all the way by fellow passengers, who handed her over on arrival, 'people were extraordinarily kind'. At Grand Central station a shopkeeper refused to take any money from this redhead, insisting she was an Irish 'colleen'.

Some marriages did not last and unhappy girls scraped together or were sent the fare home, the reality of her husband's homeland not measuring up to his glowing description. 'Some got a shock when they got to the States and found they were to live in a shack, but others were pleasantly surprised to find they had married into money.' 'I met one girl who went home to England because her husband was too wealthy, and had done nothing but play golf since his discharge two years earlier.' Other girls were so desperately homesick that they did not return from a visit home. Surprisingly though, most girls did stick it out, the divorce rate for GI brides being no higher than that of any other group. Some threw themselves enthusiastically into the new way of life, to be more American than the Americans. Others held on grimly to their 'Britishness', resisting forever the merest hint of an American accent. What did evolve was an enormous upsurge in travel across the Atlantic Ocean. The Transatlantic Brides and Parents Association, formed in the immediate post-war period to facilitate such travel and provide a point of contact for the girls, still thrives. The pages of the Association's journal have long reported golden weddings.

There is no doubt that this exodus of some 70,000 GI brides, and the many more that were to follow, contributed to the Americanisation of Britain and the popularisation of transatlantic travel. From early on the wives and children went home as often as circumstances allowed, and usually without their husbands. One girl went home for her twenty-first birthday, two years after arriving in the USA, and was sorely tempted to stay there. Once she had children she felt more anchored to her adopted country, but was forever torn between the two. Others reacted differently: 'I was never really homesick, I was an only child and very lonely. I had so much more in physical comfort than in England.' Visits home seemed to be every three or four years, especially when there were children to be shown off to grandparents. With the growth of cheaper air travel the movement was as often east to west, and ever-increasing numbers of British people became familiar with the American way of life.

Many American servicemen had kept in touch all along with the friends they had made in Britain. Shirley Thomas writes, 'Both the American boys wrote to us after they left for France, and the Corporal kept in touch even after he went back home. Then he was married and his wife kept writing and we had photographs of his children sent to us with Christmas cards and presents. One of his daughters came to visit when she was on a tour, and he and his wife came to see us a few years later. Sadly his wife died, but he managed to come over again by himself some years ago. I have taken over the correspondence since my mother died three years ago.' Similarly, 'I later visited two of them in the USA at different times. My parents had correspondence with some servicemen until they died.' 'After the war Hugh wrote to my parents. He married Lois and they had three children. They kept in touch until 1993 when my mother passed away (Hugh had died in 1982). After my mother's death I started writing to Lois who is now 75. We are in touch two or three times a year.' Another long-term friendship began with a church appeal for Christmas hospitality in 1944. The families are still in contact and each has visited the other, as have their respective children. One family was unable, until 1979, to visit the GI who had spent so much time in their home during the war. He died in 1981, and they then visited his widow. Seemingly it is never too late to seek old friends. In 2000 the Royston newspaper published a request from a GI who had been based at Steeple Morden in 1944. The paper printed a photograph taken at that time, and within a short time the veteran of eighty-one was talking over the phone to the 'young lad', now sixty-four. After the war, in the USA, the mothers of the young men who were welcomed into British homes felt they could not do enough for those women who had 'mothered' their sons at such a difficult period in everybody's life. 'When my mother visited me the first time she was overwhelmed with expensive gifts and hospitality from the mothers of the two GIs who come from my husband's home town, and had used our house as their home from home.'

But there are other legacies of the friendly invasion that remained hidden for years. Pam Winfield, who initiated TRACE, the Transatlantic Children's Enterprise, has done a great deal of research into the subject of the babies they left behind. Until the Children's Act of 1973 it was not possible for an adopted child to discover his or her progenitors. After the Act adoptees were faced with an agonising choice; some of those who did track down their parents were to discover that the father had been an American serviceman. It was not just adopted children who discovered that all was not as it seemed. The father did not have to be named on wartime birth certificates, and babies born to unmarried girls were frequently absorbed into the family as the offspring of a married sister or grandmother. That was when the family closed ranks to protect the mother and child. When it did not, the pregnant girl took herself to a suitable lying-in hospital and either gave the baby up for adoption or brought it up by herself, giving the impression that the child's father had been killed in action. If the child was coloured a charitable home was usually the sole option. For the married woman it was almost worse, especially if the husband had been serving overseas during the crucial period. Some men did accept the child as their own, some took the child in but always treated it as an outsider, some just 'made the wife and child's life hell'.

Not all these expectant mothers had been callously deserted, some of the fathers-to-be had never been told and others were judiciously 'shipped out' by their commanding officers. Some men, of course, were already married, but met their obligations nonetheless: one such supported his illegitimate daughter until her eighteenth birthday. Surprisingly, there were women who refused offers of marriage, not wanting to live in the USA. Pam Winfield quotes instances of married girls who never joined their husbands because the wife's parents, usually the mother, intercepted and destroyed communications from the GI husband, not wanting daughter and grandchild to leave the country.

There have been many stories in recent years of these children attempting to track down their fathers. Some failed altogether, while in other cases now elderly men simply did not want to be reminded of that particular part of their past and never answered enquiries. Happily, there were those who did make contact with positive results. In 1945 Lawrence Leopold, a GI stationed in Northern Ireland, went back to the USA to set up home for his British wife and child. Her family persuaded her not to join him, and it was not until his grandson Mark needed to consult his father's birth certificate that the truth was discovered. He instituted a search and then had to tell his own father: 'I'm sure it is a hell of a shock to discover that your dad is still alive after 45 years.' He found his grandfather, who had eventually remarried (as had his first wife) and was very warmly welcomed by this second family. 'From that time on our family spanned the Atlantic.' Another recently brought-to-light daughter in East Anglia bears a striking resemblance to her hitherto unknown GI father. That some of these searches have ended joyfully is a great credit to the ex-GI's American family who have welcomed the newcomer with open arms. For others it has been a saga of frustration ending in misery; perhaps better to let sleeping dogs lie.

CHAPTER 10

Remembrance

The fiftieth anniversary souvenir map published by the East Anglia Tourist Board in 1992 lists 126 airfields occupied at one time or another by the 8th or 9th Air Forces between 1942 and 1945. Most of these have long since reverted to the original farmland, but on very many of these sites, tucked away in a corner, there will be a memorial stone, a wooden gate or a plaque dedicated to the memory of the men who served there. Sometimes it is a memorial window located in the village church, or perhaps a clock or commemorative seat on the village green, which serves as a reminder of that particular American occupation. On a housing estate built in the early 1960s in Wallingford in Berkshire there are two avenues, Wallace and Andrew, named after the pilot and co-pilot who stayed aboard their crippled bomber to steer it away from the village as the rest of the crew baled out. It is always very moving to read these memorials and consider the lives lost or ruined on the missions flown from that place. At the entrance to the spectacular memorial of a Mustang propeller at Steeple Morden are two small beds of tulips, which have a special significance as they are in memory of a 355th pilot shot down near Buren in Holland and buried there. A local tulip grower developed and named a cerise tulip in his memory, and there is always a wreath from the Dutch Resistance on significant days. For the returning veterans it must sometimes be heartbreaking. The brochure for the fiftieth anniversary Grand Reunion in 1992 lists seventy-five such memorials in East Anglia alone.

After the war it may be that quite a number of veterans joined the American Legion but probably most did not, being glad to wash their hands of the entire military experience. It is more as the years pass, as they become grandfathers rather than fathers, that men look to the past. While they obviously recall the horrors and discomforts, it is the camaraderie, probably never experienced since, which is most remembered. Friendship is not a strong enough word to express the empathy felt by men who have fought together: 'My husband never got over his Lieutenant dying in his arms.' Whatever the motivation, most wartime units now have a Veterans Association in the USA. What is more astonishing is how

Pilots grouped around a Mustang somewhere in Kent. The friendships that developed between these young men while they were on British soil can be clearly seen in their faces. (Kent Messenger)

many bodies dedicated to the various American units now exist in this country. Organisations such as Friends of the Second Air Division, Friends of the Eighth (FOTE) and Buddies of the Ninth (BOTNA), let alone the myriad of individual airfield commemorative associations.

It is these associations, together with support and funding from their sister organisations in the USA, that have created the quite astonishing rash of small airfield museums now in existence. To quote the handbook of one such group: 'The 94th Bomb Group Association exists to perpetuate the memory of the comrades of the 94th and their close links to the local people around Bury St Edmunds.' Besides the restoration of the Rougham airfield control tower, the association 'has a partnership with St Edmundsbury Borough Council for the maintenance and upkeep of parts of the Appleby Memorial Garden in the Abbey Gardens in Bury St Edmunds. The Council maintains the memorials in the Rose Gardens using funds provided by the Association.'

The memorial to the 355th FG at Steeple Morden. (L.W. Millgate)

The control tower, part of the museum of the 100th BG at Thorpe Abbotts. (Author)

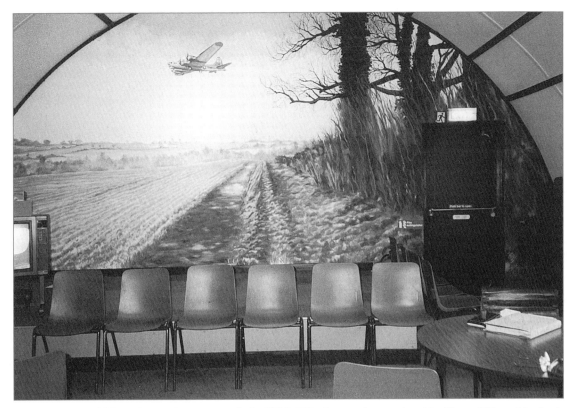

The reconstructed Nissen hut at the museum of the 100th BG; the mural was painted by Teresa Gibson. (Author)

Or the 447th Bomb Group Association, 'formed in 1982 with a view to raising sufficient funds to erect a Memorial to the 447th Bomb Group', which holds fundraising events, provides guides to the airfield at Rattlesden and regularly visits Madingley American Military Cemetery to place flowers on the graves of the twenty-two men of the 447th buried there. FOTE was formed in 1972 'by a nucleus of individuals interested in preserving the history of the United States 8th Air Force'. BOTNA appeared in the early 1980s. The memorial museum of the 100th BG is a particularly outstanding achievement: 'The story of our project to restore the Control Tower and open it to the public can be traced back to September 1977 when a number of 100th BG Association veterans returned to Thorpe Abbotts. The tower, like most of the remaining buildings was in a derelict state. The possibility of restoring the building was mentioned, and during the following weeks a small group of enthusiasts gathered to consider the idea.' This is a typical tale of local enthusiasts working with the veterans to rebuild and restore at least some of the airfield they once knew. The

Return of the 355th veterans. (Vince Hemmings)

The Wall of the Missing at the American Cemetery and Memorial, Madingley, Cambridgeshire. (Author)

The Honour Guard at Madingley. (Vince Hemmings)

re-created tower at Thorpe Abbotts was dedicated on 25 May 1981 by the ex-Gp Adt Maj Varian, and has since expanded into an excellent museum site run very efficiently by local devotees with plenty of help from the veterans.

The story of the conception and creation of the 100th ('Bloody Hundreth') Museum is characteristic of many dotted about the flat countryside of eastern Britain. On a grander scale is the permanently staffed 2nd Air Division USAAF Memorial Library in Norwich, and the Norfolk and Suffolk Aviation Museum tucked away at Flixton in Suffolk (which also incorporates the RAF Bomber Command Museum, and that of the Royal Observer Corps). Grandest of all is the American Air Museum at the Imperial War Museum, Duxford; a truly magnificent display dominated by a post-war B-52, its smaller forerunners nestled under its great wings. At the entrance to the site are fifty-two panels of glass upon which are engraved in miniature the outline of every plane lost in operations from Britain; there are 7,031 such etchings. Go to any of these museums on any day and be astonished by the number of visitors and the level of interest. If you are lucky you may bump into a veteran who might, if he chooses, fill in the details. Mostly, they just want to wander round by themselves; at

Duxford they are easily spotted, usually sporting a baseball cap and walking with that relaxed American gait.

Many new friendships have formed between the local people, young as well as old, and the American groups with whom they are constantly in touch, exchanging visits and information on an almost daily basis. In the USA the survivors – for their numbers are dwindling – keep contact through newsletters, annual reunions and organised trips to Britain. To quote one American veteran: 'I still think it's ironic that you could invite us back for a reunion when we were so obnoxious the first time.' It is as if nobody wants to let go.

The consequences of that friendly invasion are not just in memorial stones and museums, with a surprising number of Americans having settled here permanently – a Retired Officers Association exists in Suffolk. Some, of course, served here in the years following the Second World War, and indeed still do, but many first came between 1942 and 1945. Alan Channing of the 355th FG settled in Britain, where his British widow still lives: they brought up their children here, and he is buried here; at Steeple Morden there is a memorial gate in his name. Then there are the veterans who, in deference to their long-ago British brides, have elected to retire in this country. Others stayed on in the American armed forces and were posted back to the British Isles; their children were perhaps educated and married over here, so there is that enticement to stay rather than return to the USA. Others stay simply because they prefer it; Fred Goldman – semi-permanently based in London – lists his reasons: 'Aside from the cultural splendours of the city we find that its citizens are greatly more amiable, even to strangers and foreigners. Respect for pedestrians is a major plus, Zebra crossings would be useless in America.' This Anglophile is enchanted by the public parks, pubs ('rather than the characterless nature of American drinking emporia'), the proximity of the countryside, the general accessibility of everything 'and a host of little things'.

If we are looking for a postscript to the Anglo-American experience during the Second World War it can be found at Madingley, 3 miles from Cambridge. Here, set in glorious countryside, is the American Military Cemetery, the final resting place for 3,811 men, a small fraction of those who lost their lives in the European Theatre of Operations. On a wall of Portland stone are inscribed the names of 5,126 Missing in Action. It has never really ended. In June 2000 two bodies were recovered from the River Stour off Wrabness shore. It is said that the two pilots stayed on board their B-17 to steer it away from the town of Harwich, while the seven other members of the crew bailed out.

Sic transit gloria mundi.

Bibliography

Arbib, Robert, Jnr. *Here We are Together*, London, Longmans, Green & Co., 1946

Bodleian Library. *Over There; Instructions for American Servicemen in Britain, 1942*, University of Oxford, 1994

Burton, Lesley. *D-Day, Our Great Enterprise*, Gosport, Gosport Printing, 1993

Butcher, Harry C. *My Three Years with Eisenhower*, New York, Simon & Schuster, 1946

Caine, Philip D. *American Pilots in the RAF*, New York, Brassey's, 1993

Cartwright, Tony. *A Streetful of Sad Sacks*, Sawston, self-published, 1992

Colville, John. *The Fringes of Power, Downing Street Diaries 1939–45*, London, Hodder & Stoughton, 1986

Costello, John. *Love, Sex and War*, London, Pan Books, 1986

Craven, W.F and Cate, J.L. (eds). *The Army Air Forces in World War II*, vols I and II, University of Chicago Press, 1976

Crosby, Harry H. *A Wing and a Prayer*, London, Robson Books, 1998

D   Michael (ed.).
    1976

Day, Roger. *Ramsbury at War*, Hungerford, Roger Day, 1999

Downes, Michael. *Oundle's War*, Oundle, Nene Press, 1995

Freeman, Roger A. *The Mighty Eighth*, London, Military Book Society, 1973

Gardiner, Juliet. *Over Here*, London, Collins & Brown, 1992

Hale and Turner. *The Yanks are Coming*, Kent, Midas Books, 1983

Hastings, Max. *Overlord*, London, Pan Macmillan, 1993

Hoyt, Edwin P. *The GI's War*, New York, Da Capo Press, 1988

Kennett, Les. *The American Soldier in World War Two*, New York, Charles Scribnor, 1987

Leutze, James (ed.). *The London Journal of General Raymond E. Lee*, Boston, Little, Brown & Co., 1971

Longmate, Norman. *The GIs. The Americans in Britain 1941–1945*, London, Hutchinson, 1975

McClaine, Ian. *Ministry of Morale*, London, George Allen & Unwin, 1979

McLachlan, Ian and Zorn, Russell J. *8th Air Force Bomber Stories*, Somerset, Patrick Stephens, 1991

Millgate, Helen (ed.). *Mr Brown's War*, Stroud, Sutton Publishing, 1998

Nicolson, Harold (ed. Nigel Nicolson). *Diaries & Letters 1939–45*, London, Collins, 1967

O'Neill, William L. *A Democracy at War*, New York, Macmillan, 1993

Panter-Downes, Mollie. *London War Notes 1939–1945*, London, Longman, 1972

Pogue, Forrest C. *George C. Marshall – Ordeal and Hope 1939–1942*, London, Macgibbon & Kee, 1966

Raymond, Robert S. *A Yank in Bomber Command*, USA, Pacifica Press, 1998

Reynolds, David. *Rich Relations*, London, HarperCollins, 1995

Ruppenthal, Roland G. *Logistical Support of the Armies*, Washington DC Military History Dept, 1953

Sheridan, Dorothy (ed.). *Among You Taking Notes – the Wartime Diary of Naomi Mitchison*, Oxford, Oxford University Press, 1986

Sherwood, Robert E. *The White House Papers of Harry L. Hopkins*, Vol. 1, London, Eyre & Spottiswode, 1948

Smith, Graham. *Cambridgeshire Airfields in the Second World War*, Newbury, Countryside Books, 1997

——. *Suffolk Airfields in the Second World War*, Newbury, Countryside Books, 1997

Smith, Graham. *When Jim Crow Met John Bull*, London, I.B. Taurus & Co., 1987

Summersby Morgan, Kay. *Past Forgetting*, London, Collins, 1977

Wells, Ken. *Steeple Morden Strafers 1943–45*, Baldock, Herts, Egon Publishers, 1994

Winfield, Pam. *Bye Bye Baby*, London, Bloomsbury, 1992

Handbooks of the 93rd and 100th Group Memorial Museums